Portrait of a People

The Church of the Brethren at 300

Carl Desportes Bowman

Foreword by Donald B. Kraybill

Afterword by Jeffrey A. Bach

Brethren Press

Library of Congress Cataloging-in-Publication Data

Bowman, Carl Desportes, 1957-
    Portrait of a people : the Church of the Brethren at 300 / Carl Desportes Bowman ; foreword by Donald B. Kraybill ; afterword by Jeffrey A. Bach
        p. cm.
    Includes bibliographical references.
    Summary: "Analyzes the data gleaned from a statistical survey of members of the Church of the Brethren, a Protestant denomination who celebrated its 300th anniversary in 2008. Provides sociological and theological reflection as it relates to the denomination's past, present, and future" –Provided by publisher.
    ISBN: 978-0-87178-085-0
1. Church of the Brethren. I. Title.

BX7821.3.B69 2008
286'.5--dc22

                                    2008006758

12 11 10 09 08   1 2 3 4 5 6

Printed in the United States of America

This book is one of several Brethren Press publications displaying the mark of the 300th anniversary of the Brethren (1708-2008). It represents the theme "Surrendered to God, Transformed by Christ, Empowered by the Spirit."

For Laura and her brother,
Jack Desportes (1954 - 2005),
who asked questions
that wouldn't occur
to the rest of us.

Contents

Foreword

The 300th anniversary of Brethren beginnings offers a special opportunity not only to celebrate our heritage but also to assess who we are and where we are headed. The Brethren Member Profile provides an excellent mirror to view ourselves at this milestone on the Brethren journey that began in 1708 near the German village of Schwarzenau. Would Sister Joanna Kipping, Brother Alexander Mack, and the other six Brethren who were baptized in the Eder River in the late summer of 1708 recognize their spiritual kin today?

The 2006 Brethren Member Profile is the largest repository of information on the beliefs, attitudes, and behaviors of members of the Church of the Brethren. It has been gathered in a systematic fashion from a representative sample of members across the country. Carl Bowman's 1985 survey of 990 Brethren laid the foundation for this study, which tapped the views of 1,826 members. There have been many other surveys on specific topics by various groups over the years, but none have been as comprehensive or grounded in the rigors of survey methods as the 2006 Brethren Member Profile.

Respondents to the study report their views of the Bible, abortion, missions, eternal life, divorce, Jesus and salvation, and dozens of other issues. Women and men, laity and ordained, young and old, report how often they pray, read the Bible, watch television, use the Internet, exercise, and fly the American flag. Respondents also share their view of the church, their district conference, and various Brethren agencies. The responses from these 1,826 members offer a detailed description of typical Brethren beliefs and practices in Brethrenland across America.

Individual members circulate in a network of like-minded Brethren—in our local congregations or with associates in organizations such as the Brethren Revival Fellowship, Association of Brethren Caregivers, On Earth Peace, Voices for an Open Spirit, denominational and district committees, and college alumni associations. Our niche in these networks offers each of us *one* view of Brethren life from *one* vantage point in a particular circle of friends. The results of the churchwide Brethren Member Profile provide us the big picture—an overarching portrait of members across the entire church.

The 1,826 respondents were selected in a scientifically representative fashion from 106 congregations across all regions of the country. In this sense they represent and speak for all members of the Church of the Brethren. Their views tell our collective story as we pass by the 300-year milestone in our journey. At the back of the book is the bonus of a complete listing of responses to every question in the survey, including ones that are not discussed in the text.

There's something for everyone in the results. Depending on one's perspective and personal views there will be some things to cheer about and other results to weep about. Some of the findings affirm the direction of the church, while others provide challenges, and still others will raise concerns. One thing is certain: The survey numbers will not provide simple answers to our big questions. What the numeric descriptions of Brethren views and practices will do, however, is raise many interesting questions, and that is the blessing of such a comprehensive study.

Sociologists and historians such as Bowman provide us an enormous service by gathering information that helps us pinpoint the critical issues facing the church, but it's up to pastors, denominational leaders, and ordinary members to formulate responses to these challenges.

The results focus helpful issues and questions. The answers will not be found in the study, however, or in the book. Rather the answers will emerge out of conversations in congregations and in networks across the church as we discern the mind of the spirit of Jesus for the future of the church.

We are indebted to Carl Bowman for his tireless efforts to gather and analyze these results and to present them in a lively and interesting text. Some numerical reports of survey information are boring and dull; fortunately that's not the case here. This is an interpretive report, not an academic treatise. The big academic words and jargon of sociology are missing. In the pages that follow, Bowman crafts a fascinating story that describes the creases and the smiles on the Brethren face as we peer into the mirror at the beginning of the 21st century.

This is a story every member of the Church of the Brethren should read so that all of us are prepared to join in the conversation—a conversation that calls for discernment, guided by the spirit of Christ, as we shape the next steps in our journey, and as we continue the work of Jesus peacefully, simply, together.

Donald B. Kraybill
The Young Center for Anabaptist and Pietist Studies
Elizabethtown College

Acknowledgments

The Brethren Member Profile 2006 is a nationally representative survey of Church of the Brethren members 18 years of age and older. Based at Elizabethtown College's Young Center, the survey was supported financially by Mennonite Mutual Aid, Bridgewater College, Elizabethtown College, Bethany Theological Seminary, the Church of the Brethren General Board, the Association of Brethren Caregivers, Brethren Benefit Trust, On Earth Peace, and various private contributors. The Brethren Member Profile 2006, which I directed, is part of a larger Church Member Profile project that included surveys of the Mennonite Church USA and the Brethren in Christ. Donald B. Kraybill served as senior project director for the collective effort. The staff and volunteers of the Young Center deserve much of the credit for the success of the survey, since they assumed responsibility for the daily, labor-intensive activities involved in fielding it. Key members of the General Board staff in Elgin, as well as representatives of the faculty at Bethany Theological Seminary, provided helpful feedback to early drafts of the questionnaire. Donald Kraybill, Conrad Kanagy (director of the Mennonite Member Profile) and I worked collaboratively over several months to conceptualize and bring the project to fruition, but the final responsibility for the questionnaire is mine. Wendy McFadden, publisher of Brethren Press, has been tremendously supportive of this effort, and displayed remarkable patience when patience was required. Phillip C. Stone, president of Bridgewater College, graciously granted a sabbatical leave of absence, without which my involvement would have been impossible.

Carl Desportes Bowman
Bridgewater College
September 2007

Chapter 1 | **Introduction**

Three hundred years ago, in 1708, eight religious radicals in the German village of Schwarzenau formed a community of Christian brothers and sisters, calling them their "Brethren." With the New Testament as their guide, the practices of the earliest Christians as their anchor, and both spiritual awakening and outward obedience as their passions, these *neu Taüfer* soon grew from eight to several hundred members. By the mid-1830s, they had transplanted to another continent, established multiple settlements, weathered various disputes, and struggled to preserve love, unity, and faithfulness. It wasn't easy.

Two hundred years ago, in 1808, the Brethren still spoke German and were still on the move. They had fanned across southern Pennsylvania and Maryland, through Virginia, and into the Carolinas. They had crossed the Alleghenies into Kentucky, Ohio, Indiana, and even Missouri. Along the way, they encountered Native Americans, grappled with "strange teachings" in remote areas, shunned military service and the slave trade, required elders to wear beards and members to forgo fashion, prohibited selling liquor in quantities of a quart or larger, and agreed to shake hands with Brethren who had been placed in "avoidance," as long as nothing more familiar transpired. Love, unity, and obedience remained treasured ideals that were both nurtured and defined by a "Yearly Meeting," but the reality of individuals in congregations was more untidy.

One hundred years ago, in 1908, the Brethren were spread across the world. Small missions had been established in Sweden and Denmark, a larger one in India, and the first Brethren missionaries were arriving in China. More Brethren lived west of the Alleghenies than east. Ohio and Indiana accounted for more Brethren than Maryland and Virginia. And yet, in spite of the fact that their numbers had swelled to 80,000 they continued to print a tract claiming that "there is rarely found so large a body of religious people so closely united on the doctrines and principles to which they hold." Annual Meeting was partially responsible for this; its decisions were generally considered obligatory for members of the denomination. Yet in spite of this, or perhaps in part because of it, Brethren were engaged in their own internal culture war over whether they should remain distinct from other Protestant denominations, and in what ways. Plain dress, long a Dunker norm, was one sticking point, but there were many others. Paying ministers was restricted and contested. Voting in national elections was both frowned upon and cherished. Many things were changing, including the dropping of the words "German" and "Baptist" from the official church name—leaving only the word "Brethren," or more completely, "Church of the Brethren" (although "Dunkard Brethren" had been the wording recommended to Annual Meeting). Brethren who sought an alternative to secular (viz. wayward) educational institutions invested heavily in establishing their own colleges. Books and periodicals were churned out by the Brethren Publishing House at a prodigious rate, reflecting the spirit of the age.

But that was 100 years ago. What of the Brethren today? What can we say about them? Well, few today would echo the phrase about "so large a body . . . so closely united." In fact, you would be hard pressed to find any-one who describes the Church of the Brethren as "so large a body," much less "so closely united." Many loosely invoke the Anabaptist identity when they think about the Brethren, but this is partially wishful thinking and partially a clever way of saying Brethren are "sort of like the Mennonites"— which, though true, isn't entirely satisfying to anyone who acknowledges it. A recent study of the American religious landscape from Baylor University classifies the Brethren as evangelical, even though the Brethren seminary is in a cooperative relationship with the Quakers, whom the same study clas-sifies as mainline.[1] Some speak of the Brethren as multicultural and open, while most Brethren congregations exhibit an ethnic multiculturalism no more diverse than the shades of suntan on white skin. And openness is often tucked beneath a blanket of rural American culture and Brethren tradition. Still, much cultural diversity does exist among today's Brethren, though it is often more closely tied to regional, urban-rural, educational, and social class differences than to race or ethnicity.

Despite the difficulty of the challenge, this brief book will try to describe the Brethren as they really are during the first decade of the 21st century. Such a description is always more aspiration than accomplishment, and 21st-century realities are fluid enough that any portrayal, as accurate as it may be, is not only incomplete, but involves reduction and distortion. Even so, it is a wonderful challenge to try. An advantage of the present work is that its summaries and interpretations are kept in check by the discipline of survey data. While survey data reveal anything but the whole truth, they at least originate outside of the mind of the writer. Sometimes the findings correspond to the principles and hopes of the researcher, generating a quiet smile in the writing, and sometimes they paint a picture in a completely different color than the researcher had hoped.

The survey that grounds this portrait of the Brethren at their 300th birthday is the Brethren Member Profile 2006, directed by the author and conducted by Elizabethtown College's Young Center for Anabaptist and Pietist Studies.[2] Funding for the study was graciously provided by a variety of sources, most notably Mennonite Mutual Aid, the agencies of the Church of the Brethren, Bridgewater College, and Elizabethtown College. All of the findings reported in the following pages are grounded in a nationally representative sample of over 1,800 Church of the Brethren members who graciously interrupted their lives long enough to complete an 18-page questionnaire covering a broad spectrum of topics, from the abstract and political to the tangible and personal. The data were collected within a three-month period during the spring of 2006.

Anyone who knows survey research knows that response rates for such a survey—delivered to randomly selected individuals through the mail—are often low. Generally, a 50 percent response is considered excellent. Our confidence in the Brethren Member Profile is buoyed by the fact that two-thirds of the approximately 3,000 sampled members completed the lengthy questionnaire. This response rate far surpasses the typical response to such a survey, and is exceeded only by groups of, yes, Mennonites, who were sampled for a parallel study.

Our meticulous sampling and high response rate ensure that the profile contained in these pages is more than the story of the individuals who responded to the survey. It is our best estimate of the way *all Brethren* would have responded had every member nationwide completed the questionnaire. You will not always agree with my interpretation, which is intended to challenge. For this reason I have included the entire questionnaire and exact percentage distribution for each question on pages 103-146. In many ways, this report of the data in their original format is as important as my own narrative summary.

Do not miss the questionnaire. As you read it, ask yourself how you would have responded to each question; why you would have answered as you did; and how your response compares to those of other Brethren. My hope is that this will give you "something to chew on," as the old Brethren used to say, as you develop your own interpretations of past trends and future directions for the church.

Chapter 2 | Where are the Brethren?

In 2005, there were 129,837 members of the Church of the Brethren in the United States dispersed among 1,053 congregations. The vast majority of these members and congregations were located in small to medium-size towns and cities or in rural areas. Only 3 Brethren congregations of every 100—about 35 altogether—can be classified as urban or ethnic. Philadelphia, Chicago, Los Angeles, Baltimore, Miami, and Washington are the major urban centers with Brethren congregations. About half of the urban-ethnic congregations are Hispanic, with about half of those located in Puerto Rico. Additionally, about a half-dozen African American congregations and several active Haitian and Korean congregations are included in this group. In spite of these congregations, though, the Brethren at their tricentennial are overwhelmingly white, and generally located in non-urban settings. This is a denominational reality that consistently falls short of the hopes of many Brethren.

Brethren today are scattered across the entire nation, but little beyond. The foreign missionary movement of the late 19th and early 20th centuries had an enduring impact, but the 21st-century vestiges of it—most prominently the Church of the Brethren in India and Ekklesiyar Yan'uwa a Nigeria—are organizationally separate from the Church of the Brethren in the United States. More recent missions have been established in Brazil, the Dominican Republic, and Haiti. The Church of the Brethren in Puerto Rico has taken much of the initiative in the Dominican and Haitian work.

In 2005, Church of the Brethren congregations existed in 38 of the continental United States, plus the District of Columbia and Puerto Rico. In spite of this broad geographic dispersion, over half of the membership (51 percent) resides in either Pennsylvania or Virginia. The neighboring states of Maryland and West Virginia account for another 12 percent, so nearly two-thirds of the denomination's members (63 percent) live in an eastern enclave of just four states. The remaining 37 percent are distributed among 34 states, the most prominent being Ohio (11 percent), Indiana (8 percent), and Illinois (3 percent).

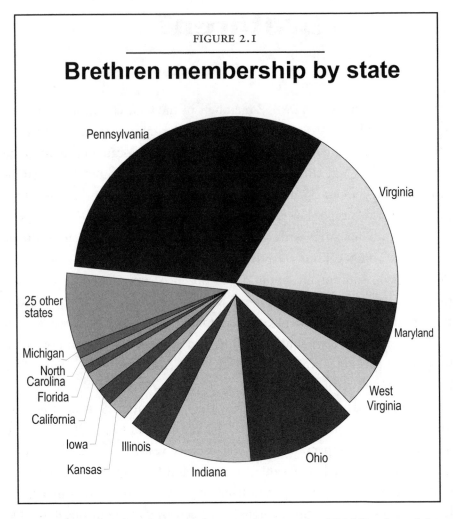

FIGURE 2.1

Brethren membership by state

The geographic distribution of respondents to the 2006 Brethren Member Profile closely mirrors the denominational geography depicted in figure

2.1. Every congregation in the denomination had a chance of being selected, with the probability being determined by the size of the congregation. Figure 2.2 depicts the precise locations of the congregations whose members participated in the survey. Were we to map the geographic coordinates of every Church of the Brethren congregation in the United States, the distribution of dots on the map would look much the same.

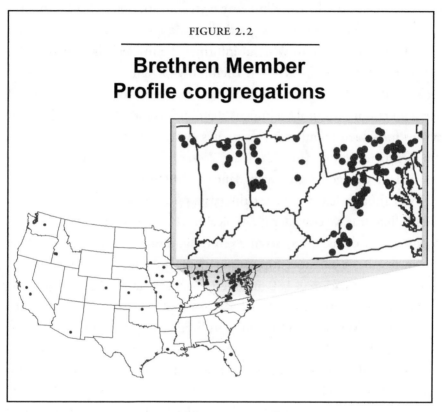

FIGURE 2.2

Brethren Member Profile congregations

The location of congregations in 2006 strongly reflects the historical patterns of migration and settlement of 18th- and 19th-century Brethren, who spread across southern Pennsylvania, migrated south through the western part of Virginia, and then followed the Ohio River into southwestern Ohio and northwest toward Chicago. The development of the railroads spurred them on through the central plains and to points farther westward, leaving an important scattering of congregations west of the Mississippi, but without the dense concentrations that still characterize the eastern states.

The typical Brethren congregation, if one dare speak of such a thing, has about 90 members, with about 60 attending worship on any given Sunday.[1] A third of Brethren congregations have 40 or fewer attending on a typical Sunday, three-quarters have 100 or fewer attending, and only one Brethren congregation out of five has a membership greater than 180. In an era of megachurches, Church of the Brethren congregations remain small. While some might classify this as failure, my own conversations with Brethren suggest that the smallness is at least partially by design. Many Brethren are more at home in congregations with an informal "family feel" in which everyone knows everyone else. Even when Brethren experience a nagging sense that "we should be reaching out and growing," the comfortable inertia of familiar faces and common history dampens their enthusiasm. Of the 1,053 congregations for which membership estimates existed in 2005, only 20 exceeded 500 members, and only one exceeded 750. Only 15 Brethren congregations reported an average worship attendance of 300 or more.

Even though it doesn't alter the basic portrait of smallness, the picture looks different if we consider the typical *member* rather than the typical *congregation*. As odd as it may seem, even though only one Brethren congregation in five has a membership greater than 180, the typical member worships in a congregation of 180 members. This is because larger congregations, though few in number, account for a disproportionately large share of the total membership. So even though most Brethren congregations (56 percent) have fewer than 100 members, these congregations account for less than a quarter of the national membership (23 percent). On average, Brethren gather with about 110 fellow worshipers on a typical Sunday, and they don't want to gather with many more; the Brethren Member Profile reveals that the ideal among today's Brethren is to belong to a congregation of about 125 active members. Few Brethren worship with fewer than 50 present, and equally few worship with more than 200.[2]

While these numbers describe typical membership and worship patterns for the church as a whole, what is "typical" varies from location to location. Pennsylvania and Florida, on average, have larger congregations, while the average worship attendance in Indiana, Ohio, Maryland, and Virginia is smaller. Worship attendance in Iowa, Illinois, California, West Virginia, and Kansas is smaller still. In general, states peripheral to the geographic center (of Pennsylvania, Maryland, Virginia, West Virginia, Ohio, and Indiana) have fewer members, dispersed among smaller congregations. Arizona, for instance, has three congregations with average attendance of 33, 43, and 50, respectively; Kentucky has four, with attendance of 5, 12, 25, and 47; and the only Colorado congregations reporting have average attendances of 24, 40, 45, and 70. Only 3 of the 22 Michigan congregations reporting have an average attendance of 70 or more. All 12 of the congregations reporting from Missouri have an average attendance of fewer than 60, with eight reporting an average attendance of fewer than 25. Of the 18 congregations reporting from California, half have 45 or fewer attending, and three-quarters have 75 or fewer. In many of these areas, congregations are not only small, but distant enough from other Brethren congregations to make the sharing of resources and programs impractical.

Chapter 3 | **Theology**

Typically classified today as a "Protestant" denomination, the Church of the Brethren at its tricentennial displays a theological diversity that differs little from many American mainline denominations. Members run the gamut from traditional evangelical to progressive. Few remnants of the Radical Pietist legacy of universal restoration or Christ-centered mysticism remain. The same is true of Anabaptist understandings of progressive salvation, community-based scriptural interpretation, the Holy Spirit, and the role of the church in preserving a disciplined body of believers that differs visibly from "the world." Some Brethren are aware of these historic emphases, and a few cling to them, but most members today are indistinguishable theologically from their Methodist, Presbyterian, or Baptist neighbors. They exhibit the same variety of beliefs. So what does this variety look like?

God

Not surprisingly, 86 percent of Brethren say that they "know God really exists and have no doubts about it." Another 11 percent admit to having doubts, but say that they "feel they do believe in God." That leaves only three percent who say they believe in a "higher power of some kind" or are uncertain about God's existence. In this general expression of belief, Brethren differ little from other American churchgoers.

The more interesting question is not whether they believe, but *how* they believe. What kind of God do Brethren envision? Half of the membership

(49 percent) worships a very engaged God, one who "controls most of the events in my daily life." But an equal number take a different view—either worshiping a less directive God (one who guides but does not control—39 percent) or expressing uncertainty about God's intervention in their lives. Only four percent state definitively that God does not intervene at all. The vast majority of Brethren (85 percent) say they feel close to God, even though these are about evenly divided between those who feel "very close" and those who feel only "fairly close." This sense of closeness is reflected in the fact that Brethren perceive their lives as purpose-driven; 93 percent say that God has a specific plan for their life. In general, then, Brethren share a sense of connection to God, even though some experience the connection more palpably and intensely than others.

More specific perceptions, however, reveal less unity. While 47 percent of Brethren, for example, believe that "God blesses all nations," about as many (43 percent) say that the statement "God has *especially* blessed America" better expresses their view.[1] Six out of 10 Brethren say that Christians and Muslims do *not* worship the same God, even though a substantial minority (38 percent) believe that they do. Thirty-six percent say that God blesses faithful Christians with financial rewards, even though the majority (63 percent) reject this notion of divine remuneration. Most Brethren feel strongly about God's gender, preferring masculine references to God. Three-quarters of today's Brethren feel positively about such references, the same proportion that say they feel negatively toward feminine references to God. Only 6 percent, less than one in 10, feel positively about feminine references to God.

Eternity

Perceptions of God are related to beliefs in the afterlife. Persons who think of God as "judge" or "king," for example, are more likely to envision eternal punishment for unbelievers, or for believers in another faith, than those who do not. Even though survey research cannot pretend to penetrate the fullness of 21st-century Brethren eschatology, it offers a glimpse into their thinking about what lies beyond.

Most Brethren, like most Christians, accept the afterlife as reality—90 percent of Brethren state definitively that "there is life after death," with only one in 10 expressing uncertainty or disbelief. Almost as many (86 percent) say that there is a real heaven where some are eternally rewarded, but somewhat fewer (75 percent) are sure there is a real hell where some are eternally punished. Nine out of 10 of these believers in hell also believe in the rapture, a time when saved persons will join Jesus and others will be "left behind." Most Brethren (73 percent) accept the traditional Christian notion that humans will see their dead loved ones in the afterlife.

Three hundred years ago, most Brethren leaders, including Alexander Mack, embraced a theology of universal restoration, a view that God's love and power were so great that all people, regardless of their beliefs, would one day be restored to God. Brethren who espoused this view also believed that Jesus himself would "come again and take vengeance with flaming fire upon those who were not obedient to his gospel,"[2] so arriving at the restoration point was clearly to be a painful process. Two centuries ago this belief persisted among some Brethren, although there is scant mention of it by the end of the 19th century. By their bicentennial, in 1908, the Brethren had essentially abandoned this legacy of their Radical Pietist heritage. Even the early Brethren who embraced universal restoration were slow to disclose it to outsiders, and were careful to distinguish it from universalism, which omitted the doctrine of divine judgment altogether.

Given their evangelical orientation, few of today's Brethren might be expected to endorse the historic doctrine of universal restoration. And the numbers are indeed few compared to the number of Brethren who believe in "eternal punishment." Even so, 27 percent of today's Brethren believe that "God's love will one day restore all souls, even non-believers, to God." What is more, only a minority (43 percent) state definitively that they do *not* believe this, with the rest saying they are not sure.

This finding contradicts other Brethren views of eternity, and probing deeper only adds to the confusion. Over half of those who say that all souls will one day be restored to God, for instance, also profess a belief in eternal punishment and the rapture. What appears to be a glaring inconsistency, in all likelihood, is a failure to fully comprehend the survey statement about universal restoration. My hunch is that many focused so completely upon the "God's love" and "restoring to God" parts of the statement, that they glossed over the words "even non-believers." So the beliefs of over half of

FIGURE 3.1

God's love will one day restore all souls, even non-believers, to God

Believe
27%

Do not believe
43%

Uncertain
30%

those who give the restoration response in figure 3.1 remain fuzzy. About 10 percent of today's Brethren, however, appear to stand outside the evangelical mainstream on this matter, rejecting the notion of eternal punishment in hell *and* expressing a belief in the universal restoration of all souls to God.

A handful of related statements elicit a variety of responses. Almost all Brethren believe that people have a soul (98 percent) and that evil is an active force in the world today (95 percent). And while 81 percent are willing to call this "evil" the Devil, only 57 percent say that the Antichrist is active in the world. The belief in angels among Brethren is strong (84 percent). And not surprisingly, just six percent of Brethren say that "humans are reincarnated and will live again on earth."

Brethren beliefs in these areas are fairly conservative, mirroring Christian beliefs that pervade the broader society.

Jesus

Since its inception, the Brethren movement has been Christ-centered. Eighteenth-century Brethren have even been described as manifesting a Christ-mysticism, an intimate longing and experience of unity with Jesus. This mysticism was related to their eager anticipation of Jesus' return at any moment. The Lord's supper at the Brethren love feast was believed to foreshadow the heavenly wedding banquet when the bridegroom (Christ) would be reunited with his bride (the church) in a great heavenly celebration. Brethren understandings of what was permitted and forbidden to Christians were anchored in the teachings of Jesus and the specific instructions given to his disciples. The Brethren Member Profile offers a glimpse of how Brethren today understand Jesus, again going beyond issues of whether they believe to explore the specific nature of that belief.

To begin with, most Brethren did *not* accept Jesus at a dramatic juncture or turning point in their lives. When asked, "Was there ever a time in your life when you accepted Christ as Savior and Lord?" fewer than half (40 percent) say, "Yes, it was a specific moment." Fifty-seven percent, on the other hand, say, "Yes, but it happened gradually over time." The study also reveals that most Brethren (73 percent) accept the orthodox view that Jesus is "fully divine and fully God." Of the remaining 27 percent, most (22 percent) say that Jesus is divine, but "not exactly God." Only five percent—one member out of 20—think of Jesus as something less than "divine."

While Brethren are united regarding Jesus' divinity, they part company on the question of Jesus' uniqueness (see figure 3.2 on page 16). Most Brethren (64 percent) embrace the traditional view that "Jesus is the only way to God and those without faith in Jesus will not be saved," but that leaves more than a third (34 percent) who believe that salvation may be extended to those who don't know Jesus. This is very similar to the number (38 percent) who believe that Christians and Muslims worship the same God.

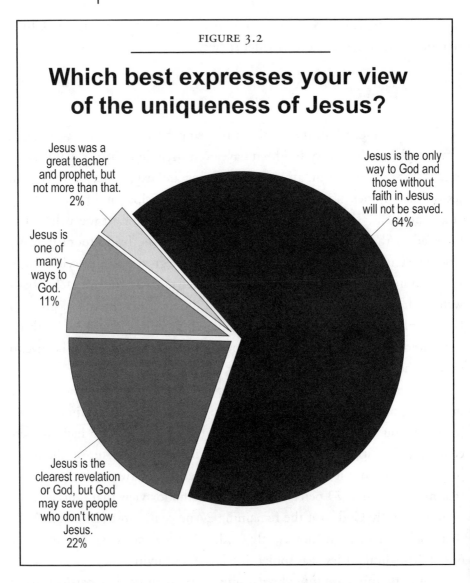

FIGURE 3.2

Which best expresses your view of the uniqueness of Jesus?

Jesus was a great teacher and prophet, but not more than that.
2%

Jesus is one of many ways to God.
11%

Jesus is the clearest revelation or God, but God may save people who don't know Jesus.
22%

Jesus is the only way to God and those without faith in Jesus will not be saved.
64%

In addition to these basic questions about Jesus' divinity and uniqueness, the Brethren Member Profile presented respondents with a list of specific statements about Jesus, instructing them to check as many as reflect their own beliefs. Some of the results are predictable. Given their baptismal confession, for example, it is not surprising that most Brethren (82 percent) think of Jesus as "their personal Lord and Savior." This is something that Brethren proclaim publicly at the point of joining the church, so we would expect a strong endorsement of this basic faith tenet.

Less predictable is the fact that only 6 out of 10 members (60 percent) marked, "I seek to be a disciple of Jesus in my daily living." This suggests that, for some, the confession of Jesus as Lord and Savior is but an abstraction, something that they affirm automatically rather than considering the concrete implications of the confession. This hunch is given greater credence when one considers that only a minority of Brethren say they have a "close personal relationship with Christ" (48 percent) or an "intimate spiritual connection with Jesus" (34 percent). The latter suggest that whatever remnants of the early Christ-centered mysticism remain are diminished after 300 years.

Given the historic doctrines of the Brethren, it is also surprising that only a minority (43 percent) say they "think of Jesus as a nonviolent peacemaker" and that they "eagerly anticipate Jesus' return to earth" (39 percent). Upon reflection, one is left with the sense that perhaps half of today's Brethren experience Jesus as a compelling presence or master, even though many more acknowledge his divinity and his divine role in a more detached way.

The Holy Spirit

Virtually all of today's Brethren (95 percent) see the Holy Spirit as active in the world. Yet when asked about their own reception of "gifts of the Spirit," the most common response is that they have personally received "none of the above" (47 percent). Of the gifts that *have* been received, the most common by far is the "baptism of the Spirit," which is claimed by 43 percent of respondents. Few, however, report having received other extraordinary gifts, such as the ability to speak in tongues (4 percent), the gift of prophecy (4 percent), the power to heal (3 percent), or the power to cast out demons (2 percent). Consistent with these findings, only 4 percent of Brethren identify themselves as "charismatic" Christians. This is put into stark relief if we recall that 6 percent of respondents to the Brethren Member Profile profess a belief in reincarnation.

Early Brethren believed that the Holy Spirit directly guided the discernment and decisions of the gathered church. Individual believers whose "inner ear" was open could hear the whisperings of the Spirit, but personal illumination had to be confirmed by the faith community to ensure that t was more than self-deception. In other words, the church was understood to be the final arbiter of the Holy Spirit's whisperings to individual Brethren.

To ensure that the church was indeed inspired of the Spirit, all decisions were reached by "unanimous consent"—a process in which all did not have to see eye to eye, but still agreed to be governed by church rulings until such time as the faith community might receive "new light" or greater wisdom. When all could not consent in this manner, deliberations had to continue until vocal dissent subsided. A spirit of individual yielding was nurtured by prayer, thereby calling upon the Spirit to lead Brethren into unity on specific matters of faith and practice. As messy as such decision making could sometimes be, spiritual unity, in which the collective voice was primary, remained the constant aspiration.

Today, Brethren play by different spiritual rules. While the gathered community is still granted a role in discerning the Spirit's leading, Brethren no longer grant it primacy. Instead, individuals are in the driver's seat, with the church relegated to a support role. In response to the question "Which statement *best* describes your view of how the Holy Spirit works?" 4 out of 10 Brethren (39 percent) leave the community out altogether, saying pointedly, "the Spirit speaks directly to individuals in a personal way." Another 5 out of 10 (51 percent) say "the Spirit speaks to individuals directly, and also through the faith community." Only 3 percent say that the Spirit speaks "primarily through the faith community," making this view even less popular among Brethren than the secular view that the Spirit is simply "another name for human insight or inspiration" (8 percent).

The Bible

Historically, the Spirit's role in leading the community was most pronounced when it came to biblical interpretation. Brethren were known as a people of the Book—they grounded their behavioral codes in scripture, their church structures and rituals in scripture, and, rather than authoring a creed, acknowledged the entire New Testament as their *rule of faith and practice*. The wording of this phrase is key: The Bible wasn't simply about historical or holy realities; it was equally a guidebook for living.[3]

More pointedly, the New Testament was considered a rule book for living and practicing one's faith; this was the straightforward way in which Brethren approached scripture. It is significant that Brethren did not refer to the entire *Bible* as their rule of faith and practice. Neither did they focus upon the fact that the entire Bible was the "literal" or "inerrant" Word of God. Such language might have raised eyebrows among the early Brethren, leaving them to wonder, What exactly does *that* mean? Rather than being "literalists" in the modern fundamentalist sense of the word, the Brethren were strong biblicists who perpetually approached the Bible with a practical query: What does this say about how we should worship, live, and be the church together? To answer this question, they turned primarily to the New Testament—precisely because it was understood to be a *new* testament, fulfilling prophecies of the old, but also differing from it. It was the *new* testament that was understood to be the foundation of the Christian faith, and within the New Testament the teachings of Jesus and activities of the early apostles were considered primary. There was thus a hierarchy of scripture, read with a straightforward and practical bent.

What of today's Brethren? On the positive side, 44 percent—nearly half—say that they read the Bible on their own at least several times a week, with half of this group saying they read the Bible daily. But another 44 percent say that they read the Bible less than once a week. In fact, 3 out of 10 members (29 percent) say they read the Bible only "several times a year," if at all. Slightly more than a third (37 percent) engage at least monthly in some form of small group worship that involves prayer or Bible study, but this leaves a majority who do not. This is a mixed profile, to be sure, but given that there are more reading their Bibles only several times a year than daily, the practice of today's Brethren falls well short of being a consistent "people of the Book."

The ways in which today's Brethren approach scripture vary considerably as well. Forty-five percent take the literalist position that the Bible is the *actual* word of God, "to be taken literally, word for word." About the same number, though (46 percent), say that the Bible is the *inspired* word of God, but that "not everything should be taken literally." The remaining 10 percent of Brethren say that the Bible is an ancient book of stories, history, and moral guidelines recorded by human authors. Ironically, a quarter (26 percent) of those who say that the Bible should be taken literally read it once a month or less, raising questions about the fit between their perception of scriptural authority and its place in their daily lives.

When asked which testament in the Bible has the "highest authority," about half of today's Brethren (49 percent) say the New Testament, which is the answer most consistent with the New Testament's designation as their rule of faith and practice. Another 46 percent say that both testaments have equal authority, while only 5 percent say that the Old Testament has greater authority. Offered an opportunity to identify their "favorite passage" of scripture, the overwhelming favorite is John 3:16, "For God so loved the world, that he sent his only begotten Son, that whosoever believeth in him should not perish, but have everlasting life" (KJV). Nearly a third of respondents cited this single verse. Another third wrote in some other verse from the New Testament, and the remaining third wrote in some passage from the Old Testament, most typically the 23rd Psalm.

Religious identity

A remaining theological issue worthy of consideration is that of religious identity. One hundred years ago, many Brethren still thought of themselves as "Dunkers," a plain people set apart from the currents of mainstream Christianity. But what of Brethren today? Do they think of themselves quite broadly as "Christians" or in more particular terms—as Pietists, Anabaptists, Fundamentalists, or some other specific category?

Given a list of 15 religious identities from which multiple terms could be selected, the most prominent identity by far is "Brethren." More than four-fifths of the membership (83 percent) say that "Brethren" describes their religious faith. In fact, 27 percent pick Brethren as the only identity of the 15 that describes their faith. After Brethren, the most commonly embraced identity is "spiritual," a term that transcends the liberal-to-conservative divide in American religious life. Not only do 40 percent of Brethren say they are "spiritual," but virtually all of these say that spiritual is one of the words that best describes their faith.

Brethren who consider themselves religious conservatives outnumber religious liberals by a four-to-one ratio. Forty-five percent self-identify as religiously conservative, 44 percent as religiously moderate, and just 11 percent as religiously liberal.

But even though conservatism, broadly speaking, is warmly embraced, the labels associated with religious conservatism are not. From the list of 15 terms mentioned above, only 15 percent of Brethren identify themselves as "evangelical"; 10 percent as "fundamentalist"; 4 percent as "charismatic"; and 2 percent as "Pentecostal." In light of their history, it is noteworthy that more Brethren self-identify as Anabaptist (19 percent) than evangelical, as mainline Protestant (14 percent) than fundamentalist, and as "Dunker" (7 percent) than as charismatic or Pentecostal.

More than half of today's Brethren (59 percent) describe themselves as "born-again" Christians, but it is likely that "born-again" has a broader meaning for Brethren than for many American Christians. An emphasis upon "spiritual rebirth," associated with adult baptism, has a three-century legacy among Brethren, a legacy that remains vibrant enough that when Brethren describe themselves as "born again" it is not at all clear that they are simply echoing the usage popular among mainstream evangelicals. Evidence to this effect is the fact that 2 out of 10 Brethren (18 percent) are "not sure" whether they would describe themselves as "born again," almost as many as those who state definitely that they are not (23 percent). Further evidence of the broader applicability of "born again" among Brethren is the fact that:

- half of "born again" Brethren accepted Christ gradually over time, rather than at a specific moment.

- 4 out of 10 "born again" Brethren express openness to the idea that God's love will one day restore everyone, even non-believers, to God.

- relatively few "born again" Brethren selected the terms evangelical (22 percent), fundamentalist (13 percent), charismatic (5 percent), or Pentecostal (3 percent) to describe their religious identity, compared with 44 percent who described themselves as spiritual, 20 percent as Anabaptist, 16 percent as "plain living," and even 11 percent who identified themselves as "mainline Protestants."

- 57 percent of "born again" Brethren describe their religious views as conservative, which leaves nearly half (43 percent) who do not consider themselves religiously conservative.

- 36 percent of "born again" Brethren describe themselves as political moderates or liberals.

Even though there is evidence that born again language applies more broadly among Brethren than in the culture at large, Brethren who describe themselves as "born again" are more concerned with questions of salvation, evangelism, and conservative moral values than are Brethren who reject the born again label. And the latter—those who reject the label—elevate peace and justice concerns above many other religious issues, while "born agains" give peace concerns less *relative* prominence.

| Chapter | **Brethren**
| 4 | **connections**

Peoplehood

One hundred years ago, Dunker educator and evangelist I. N. H. Beahm carried a journal with a small *Brethren's Card* that introduced the Brethren with the words, "Be it known, that there is a people. . . ." A glance at my father's family tree, in which each of his four grandparents is a close cousin to each of the others, visually confirms what being a people meant. Among Brethren, "second-cousin" appears to have been code language for "prospective mate." Like Mennonites or Jews, Brethren of a century ago tended to marry Brethren, to center their lives in their Brethren community, and to worship in a congregation that abounded in not just spiritual brothers and sisters, but blood relatives. To this day, all I have to hear from someone is that they have family roots in the Brethren congregations of Franklin County, Virginia, to know that we are related. I may not know how or how closely, but I can speak with confidence that the connection exists. The next time we meet, they often announce that a parent or grandparent informs them that I'm their _____-cousin. So the traces of ethnic peoplehood remain to this day. There are even members, albeit few, who will say, "I don't know whether I'm Christian, but I *know* I'm Brethren," in much the same way that Jews might ground their Jewishness in ancestry rather than a faith conviction, or that a birth-Mennonite still thinks of herself as "Mennonite at heart" after 30 years of membership in a Brethren congregation.

So peoplehood was more than just a turn of a phrase. But when we consider the Brethren of today, does kinship-based peoplehood persist, or is it just a fading footprint from an ethnically tinged past? If the presence of Brethren ancestry among the members provides the answer, then the reviews are mixed. Just over half (52 percent) of today's Brethren have ancestral roots going back to at least one grandparent; they have both parents *and* grandparents who were Brethren members (see figure 4.1). If we add to this group the additional 13 percent who have either a Brethren parent *or* a grandparent, but not both, we find that 65 percent of today's Brethren (about two-thirds) have at least some Brethren ancestry. Adding to this the members with no Brethren ancestry of their own, but who married someone who was raised Brethren, increases the percentage of today's membership with a Brethren family connection to 79 percent, about four of every five Brethren. The remaining one in five reports no family connection at all, through either blood or marriage.[1]

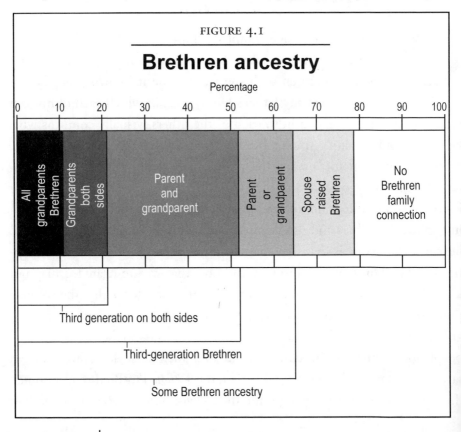

FIGURE 4.1

Brethren ancestry

Percentage

Stability

Beyond ancestry, the Brethren Member Profile reveals that 7 out of 10 members were first baptized within the Church of the Brethren, and that over half (60 percent) have never belonged to a non-Brethren congregation. The average length of membership is just over 30 years. When members *have* come to the Brethren from another denomination, it is most typically from a Methodist (20 percent), Baptist (16 percent), Lutheran (10 percent), Mennonite (5 percent), or Catholic (5 percent) background.

This portrait of religious stability is painted upon a small-town backdrop of *residential* stability. Even though approximately 80 percent of the United States population resides in urban areas, 70 percent of today's Brethren live in small towns (of fewer than 10,000 residents) or rural areas. And an even greater percentage have rural roots: 82 percent report that they were raised in small towns or rural areas. In fact, over a third (36 percent) report that they were raised on a farm. More important, perhaps, than where Brethren live is the fact that they generally stay where they are. Nearly two-thirds have lived in their present community for more than 20 years. Four of every five Brethren have lived in their present community for at least 10 years.

Annual Conference

Big Meeting—Yearly Meeting—The Brethren's Annual Meeting. The Church of the Brethren Annual Conference has had many names over the years, but whatever the name it has always been considered a family reunion of the faithful. One cannot peruse Brethren scholarship, subscribe to *Messenger*, or speak with Brethren ministers over age 50 without receiving the clear message that Annual Conference is key to understanding the Brethren.

Historical documents from the 1870s to about 1900 suggest that Brethren attended "Annual Meeting" at a rate of about 30 attendees for every 100 members nationwide. Attendance was highest, of course, when Conference was held near a center of Brethren settlement (eastern Pennsylvania or southeastern Indiana, for instance). But regardless of location, attendance was consistently high, regularly reaching 15,000 to 30,000 persons at a time when the total denominational membership ranged from 50–75,000. Scant evidence from the early 19th century suggests that Annual Conference attendance may even have exceeded the size of the Brethren membership on occasion.

Much is different today. Brethren are more encumbered by a variety of religious and secular commitments. The agricultural calendar no longer shapes the seasons of church life. Brethren are much more connected to the society at large, and have less of their identity vested in their own faith community. New modes of transportation, communications media, and the Internet have extended their social, economic, and professional worlds far beyond the localized focus of the 19th century. And the authority of Annual Conference itself pales in comparison to its authority over the lives of members a century ago. The result has been a steady decline in the proportion of Brethren attending. At the eve of the tricentennial, with national membership at approximately 125,000, attendance at the Church of the Brethren Annual Conference typically ranges from 2–4,000, which is about 2 to 3 persons for every 100 members nationwide. The number of Brethren attending is about half what it was only 30 years ago.

A Brethren remnant, it is true, still travels to Annual Conference every year, but it is equally true that the majority of Brethren do not. As a matter of fact, most Brethren *never* make the trek, regardless of location. In spite of their Brethren family ties and typical length of membership, nearly two-thirds of today's Brethren (62 percent) have never attended a Church of the Brethren Annual Conference, with the figure rising to nearly three-quarters (73 percent) among Brethren younger than 50 (see figure 4.2). Only a quarter (24 percent) have attended Conference more than once. About one member out of 5 (19 percent) has served as a delegate. And only one out of 10 (9 percent) has served as a delegate more than once.

Age comparisons suggest that the decline has occurred within the life span of today's senior citizens, for nearly half (48 percent) of those of retirement age have attended Annual Conference, compared to 27 percent of those younger than 50.[2] Clearly, if this is a "Brethren family reunion," it faces the fate of many family reunions in contemporary America: People are either too encumbered or too disinterested to show up.

In spite of the low attendance, Annual Conference elicits a generally positive response from the membership. In fact, 91 percent of those who express an opinion say that they are at least "fairly satisfied" with the program and emphases of Annual Conference. This approval rating is similar to that received by the General Board and the Brethren Service Center, yet it is artificially inflated by the fact that 40 percent of the membership express no opinion at all. While only 5 percent of today's Brethren express overt dissatisfaction with Annual Conference, less than one in 5 (19 percent) say they are "very satisfied."

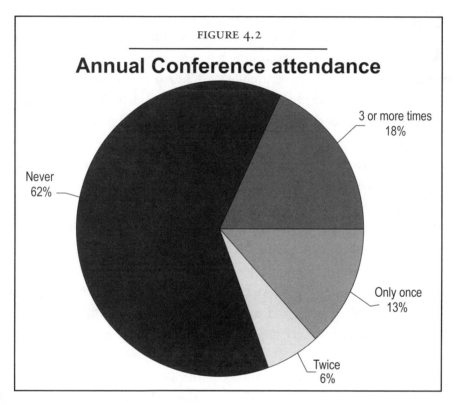

FIGURE 4.2

Annual Conference attendance

Never
62%

3 or more times
18%

Only once
13%

Twice
6%

The general portrait appears to be one of benevolent indifference. Three-quarters of today's Brethren offer the kind of opinion about Annual Conference that one gives when not particularly invested: "fairly satisfied," "not sure," or no response at all. The pattern is the same when Brethren are asked whether they agree or disagree that Annual Conference is too expensive to hold every year. Six out of 10 say "neither" or they skip the question altogether. Nearly half of the membership (45 percent) say that Annual Conference decisions and rulings are not very important to them personally, and another 42 percent say they are "fairly important," which can be given a positive or negative spin. A sizable minority of Brethren believe that con gregations should seriously consider the rulings of Annual Conference, eve though only about 10 percent believe that there should be strong sanction for congregations that fail to comply.

Other Brethren institutions

Besides Annual Conference, the Church of the Brethren offers man opportunities for involvement beyond the local level. Participatio levels vary, though, according to the activity. Forty percent of today Brethren, for example, have attended a Church of the Brethren summe camp, and nearly as many (38 percent) have attended district conference Fewer than 20 percent of all Brethren, on the other hand, have attende National Youth Conference—though the participation rate is higher for re spondents under age 35, nearly 40 percent of whom have attended. Othe denominational programs—Faith Expeditions, Christian Citizenship Sem nar, Brethren Volunteer Service, and National Young Adult Conference, t name a few—are experienced by only a small proportion of the membershi (5 percent or less in each case). Even though many of these events are short lived, their impact often extends for years, in many cases shaping vocationa and even marital decisions, as well as commitment to core Brethren values.

The national agencies and organizations of the church, of course, ar directly experienced by very few. This lack of familiarity may, in fact, be th key to understanding how Brethren responded to our questions assessin satisfaction with Brethren organizations. The most striking finding in figur 4.3 is not the percent satisfied or dissatisfied, as had been our assumption, bu the percentage of Brethren who are "unsure" what they think. This is mos notable in the case of the finance-related offices of the church, suggesting tha approximately three-quarters of the national membership have no meaningfu framework for assessing Brethren Benefit Trust, Brethren insurance plan: the Church of the Brethren Credit Union, and the like. The uncertaint level is high as well for various special interest groups, including Brethre Encyclopedia, Womæn's Caucus, Outdoor Ministries Association, Brethre Revival Fellowship, and Brethren Mennonite Council for Gay and Lesbia Concerns (now named the Brethren Mennonite Council for Lesbian, Ga

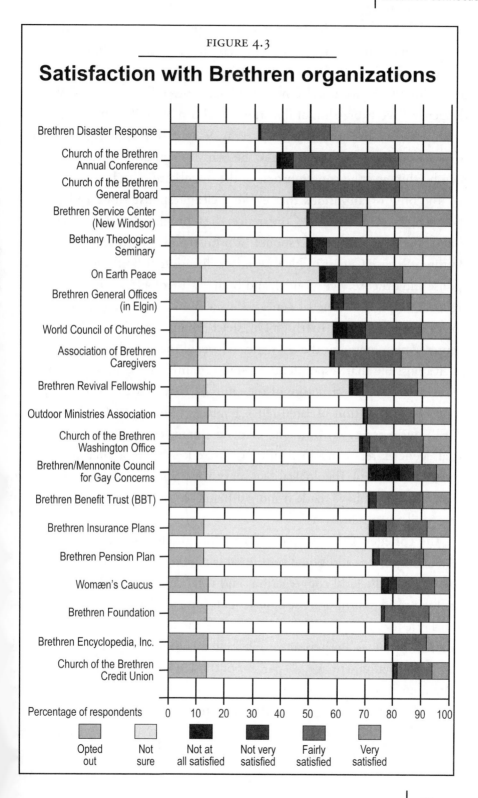

FIGURE 4.3

Satisfaction with Brethren organizations

Brethren Disaster Response

Church of the Brethren Annual Conference

Church of the Brethren General Board

Brethren Service Center (New Windsor)

Bethany Theological Seminary

On Earth Peace

Brethren General Offices (in Elgin)

World Council of Churches

Association of Brethren Caregivers

Brethren Revival Fellowship

Outdoor Ministries Association

Church of the Brethren Washington Office

Brethren/Mennonite Council for Gay Concerns

Brethren Benefit Trust (BBT)

Brethren Insurance Plans

Brethren Pension Plan

Womæn's Caucus

Brethren Foundation

Brethren Encyclopedia, Inc.

Church of the Brethren Credit Union

Percentage of respondents   0   10   20   30   40   50   60   70   80   90   100

Opted out | Not sure | Not at all satisfied | Not very satisfied | Fairly satisfied | Very satisfied

Bisexual, and Transgender Interests). In comparison, Brethren are somewhat more inclined to venture an opinion about the General Offices in Elgin, which houses three of the official agencies of the church, and the Association of Brethren Caregivers and On Earth Peace, both official agencies. Whether the generalized expression of uncertainty is born of indifference, irrelevance, or simply a lack of familiarity, we can't say. Whatever its nature, there appears to be a large awareness gap between the many organizations that relate to the membership and the consciousness of the membership itself.

The only organizations that evoke a clear response from a majority of today's Brethren are Annual Conference, the Church of the Brethren General Board, Brethren Disaster Response (a ministry of the General Board), the Brethren Service Center in New Windsor (location of Brethren Disaster Response and other service groups), and Bethany Theological Seminary. In each case, the response is one of general satisfaction. The strongest satisfaction, however, is reserved for Brethren Disaster Response and the Brethren Service Center, which represent the assistance efforts of the church.

It's possible that respondents' overall unfamiliarity is more pronounced because of a 1997 restructure of the church. That year two small organizations, the Association of Brethren Caregivers (ABC) and On Earth Peace (OEP), were separated from the General Board, eventually to become official agencies reporting to Annual Conference. Though Brethren Benefit Trust and Bethany Theological Seminary were not new, the overall change in dynamics may have made it more difficult for people to understand what seemed like new acronyms.

The colleges. Over the past century, the Brethren-related colleges have been an important additional vehicle for expanding denominational connections beyond the local congregations and rural communities in which many Brethren reside. Although the colleges continue to play an important educational role for many Brethren young people, the tendency to invoke denominational loyalty as a criterion for selecting a college is on the wane. Among Brethren of retirement age, 36 percent of those who attended college went to a Brethren-related one. By contrast, only 13 percent of Brethren under age 35 did the same. Among those who did attend a Brethren college, the most commonly attended ones have been Manchester (42 percent), Bridgewater (23 percent), and McPherson (16 percent), while Elizabethtown (10 percent)

Juniata (6 percent), and La Verne (2 percent) have been attended by relatively few. Brethren younger than 50, however, reflect different preferences, with greater numbers attending Bridgewater (31 percent) and McPherson (20 percent), and proportionately fewer attending Manchester (32 percent) and Elizabethtown (8 percent).[3]

Even though fewer than 3 percent of all survey respondents report having attended Bethany Theological Seminary, this is larger than the number for any other Brethren institution of higher education, with the single exception of Manchester College.

Messenger. Another institution that regularly weaves Brethren into their larger faith community is *Messenger* magazine. Heir to a string of Brethren periodicals dating back to Henry Kurtz's 1851 *Gospel Visitor*, the denominational monthly brings news about everything from local congregations to global programs into the homes of Brethren families. *Messenger* publishes a mix of thoughtful essays and features on a broad spectrum of topics pertaining to Christian faithfulness in the contemporary age, as well as media reviews and Bible study. Letters from members, whether positive or critical in tone, round out the mix of regular features. While some Brethren congregations pay the entire cost of the *Messenger* subscription to ensure that every member receives news about the larger church, other congregations are disinterested if not disparaging in their response to the magazine. Generally speaking, the more rural and remote the congregation, the less likely *Messenger* is to be a vital information source, which only increases the congregation's isolation from the larger Brethren fellowship.

The Brethren Member Profile suggests that approximately 30 percent of the membership receive *Messenger* at home. The percentage varies regionally, from as high as half to two-thirds of the membership in Indiana and Illinois, to about 20 percent in Virginia and West Virginia. In general, subscription rates appear higher in the Midwest and West, where Brethren experience greater isolation from other Brethren.

Brethren thickening

Whether the connection is personal ancestry, summer camp, a Brethren college, *Messenger*, or Annual Conference, Brethren connections are more than they seem. Relationships are the reservoirs of commitment, and values are transformed in conversation with others, so a brief stint in volunteer service or disaster relief is more than just a brief stint; it can nurture an enduring commitment by involving one personally in a both a legacy and a distinctively Brethren social network. The same can be said for attending Annual Conference, reading *Messenger*, or traveling to National Youth Conference. They are all agents of Brethren thickening—exposing Brethren to not only a legacy, but to what "another way of living" means at the point of the Brethren tricentennial.

Take Annual Conference. Survey research lets us examine not only rates of attendance, but also the differences between attenders and non-attenders. Frequent attenders, for instance, are four times more likely to have deep Brethren family roots than non-attenders.[4] Frequent attenders are also much more likely to express satisfaction with denominational organizations and programs. Nearly one-third (30 percent) of those who frequently attend Conference have graduated from a Brethren college, compared to about 2 percent of those who have never attended. Frequent attenders are also older, more likely to be Democrats, and more likely to see the Brethren as distinct from other Protestant denominations. They are more commonly employed in education or human services occupations and *less* likely to be employed in a variety of sales, clerical, blue collar, and transportation-related occupations.

These differences notwithstanding, the similarities between frequent Annual Conference attenders and non-attenders are also noteworthy. On issues of personal morality, for instance (premarital sex, couples living together before marriage, and the consumption of alcoholic beverages), they look virtually identical. If anything, Conferencegoers are more likely to see such things as "always wrong" than non-attenders. And frequent attenders are as likely, if not more likely, than non-attenders to say that religion and spirituality are very important in their lives and that they feel close to God.

Yet while the *intensity* of their religious commitments are similar, digging deeper reveals that the *nature* of those commitments differ. For example, compared to Brethren who have never attended Annual Conference, frequent Conference attenders are more likely to:

- impart greater authority to the New Testament than to the Old.

- think of God as offering guidance, rather than controlling the events in their lives.

- claim "spiritual," "Pietist," and particularly "Anabaptist" as elements of their religious identity.

- say that they seek to be a disciple of Jesus in their daily living.

- believe that Muslims and Christians worship the same God.

- think of Jesus as a nonviolent peacemaker.

- believe that "all war is sin."

Brethren who have never attended Annual Conference are more likely than frequent attenders, on the other hand, to:

- think of themselves as religious "conservatives."

- say that human nature is basically sinful.

- believe that God created humans in their present form at creation.

- say that Jesus is "the only way" to God.

- believe that everything in the Bible should be taken literally, word for word.

- believe that hell is a real place where humans are eternally punished, and that the Devil is a personal being who is active in our world.

- view the biblical miracles as historical facts.

- believe in the "rapture," the Antichrist, and other millenarian tenets.

So there are clear differences between these groups of Brethren. Yet these differences are better understood as alternate ways of *framing* faith than as differential *levels* of faith. Advocates of early 20th-century Brethren understandings may see the second of these two lists as a more authentic Brethren expression. Others, however, will see the first as more "Brethren" because of its focus upon the New Testament, theological openness, peace, and Christian discipleship. As we contemplate the possibility of an "Annual Conference gap," it is clear that the gap is a matter of *relative* emphases and group *averages*, rather than a stark dichotomy. Many frequent Conferencegoers ascribe to statements in the second list, and vice versa. But on average, there is greater support for the second list among those who have never been to an Annual Conference, and for the first, among frequent Conferencegoers.

Nowhere is Annual Conference more of a Brethren thickener than in the area of peace commitments. While frequent Conferencegoers and non-attenders are equally likely to describe peacemaking and nonviolence,

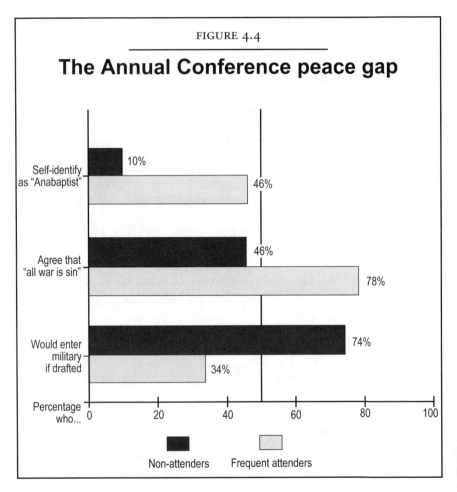

FIGURE 4.4

The Annual Conference peace gap

at least abstractly, as important faith commitments, they part company in their concrete views of war and military service. Specifically, frequent Conferencegoers align themselves much more closely than non-attenders with the traditional Brethren view that war is sin and that military service is inconsistent with Christ's teaching (see figure 4.4). Annual Conference marches protesting the Iraq war and similar events symbolically underscore the difference between frequent Conferencegoers and the rest of the denomination. In recent years, perhaps nothing symbolically captured the difference so much as moderator Paul Grout's delay of Annual Conference business because of an American flag hanging in the back of the hall. Even though there is solid Annual Conference precedent for such a stance, the action would have left many non-attenders puzzled.

Annual Conference's association with denominational commitment is also seen in other areas. Frequent Conferencegoers, for instance, are more likely than non-attenders to:

- prefer that their minister be educated at Bethany Seminary (52 percent of frequent attenders, compared to 20 percent of non-attenders)

- attend love feast at least once a year (83 percent compared to 57 percent)

- receive *Messenger* in their home (71 percent compared to 20 percent)

- say that it is *very important* that their local congregation is a part of the Church of the Brethren denomination (65 percent compared to 31 percent)

- express a strong personal commitment to the Church of the Brethren nationally (78 percent compared to 36 percent)

In short, those who are most attuned to Annual Conference, making it a regular pilgrimage, are a breed apart in the contemporary Church of the Brethren. For this small but committed minority, Annual Conference decisions, fellowship, worship, and reconnecting are an important yearly ritual, offering them a sense of shared ministry to the denomination and witness to the world. One cannot conclude that Annual Conference is the *cause* of greater commitment to the denomination, nor to its peace witness in particular, but Annual Conference and the relationships that it represents, certainly reinforce Brethren commitments in these areas. Typically speaking, frequent Conferencegoers do not take the Church of the Brethren lightly, and for them the Church of the Brethren is much larger than the activities of their local congregations.

As we consider this sense of attachment, its lack of diffusion among the general membership is cause for reflection. After all, fewer than 4 out of every 10 Brethren have ever attended Annual Conference, only 3 out of 10 (at best) subscribe to *Messenger*, and about the same number communicate a general lack of awareness about Brethren programs and agencies. It is not surprising that the majority of today's Brethren (54 percent) say they have a weak personal commitment to the Church of the Brethren nationally. Half of the membership say that "church denominations do not matter to me; one is as good as another." A majority (58 percent) say that it makes no difference whether their Sunday school materials are published by the Brethren or some other publisher. Only 29 percent say they prefer that their pastor's seminary education be from Bethany. The fact that declining denominational loyalty is a general trend in the United States makes this no less striking. In fact, today's Brethren express greater personal commitment to "the broader Christian Church" than to their own denomination. That said, their greatest loyalty is neither to the broader church nor to their denomination, but to their own congregation. Eighty-three percent say that their personal commitment to their local congregation is strong, about twice the number who say they have strong commitment to the Church of the Brethren nationally (46 percent).

Chapter 5 | **Personal faith expressions**

The personal investment of Brethren in their faith is reflected in their private devotional life. Two-thirds report that they pray privately on a daily basis, and 86 percent say that they pray privately at least several times a week (see figure 5.1). Fewer, but still a substantial number, say that on a daily basis they seek the Holy Spirit's guidance (50 percent) and pray before meals (48 percent).

One can interpret these figures from a "glass half full" or "glass half empty" perspective. Those who see the glass half empty would find further evidence in the fact that about a third of today's Brethren say grace less than once a week, and that 22 percent do it only a couple of times a year, if that often. Bible study is similarly varied, with a large number (44 percent) reading the Bible privately at least several times a week, but an equal number admitting that, at best, they do so only a few times a month. In fact, the number who read their Bible daily (22 percent) is exceeded by the number who do so less than once a month (29 percent). In this case, as in the case of grace before meals, it is difficult to say what is "typical" because Brethren are all over the map.

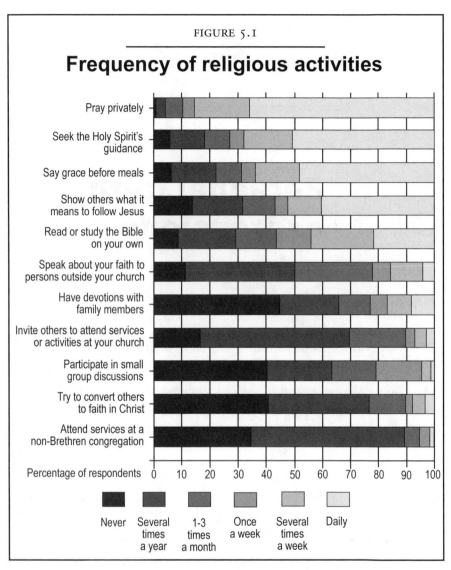

FIGURE 5.1

Frequency of religious activities

Pray privately
Seek the Holy Spirit's guidance
Say grace before meals
Show others what it means to follow Jesus
Read or study the Bible on your own
Speak about your faith to persons outside your church
Have devotions with family members
Invite others to attend services or activities at your church
Participate in small group discussions
Try to convert others to faith in Christ
Attend services at a non-Brethren congregation

Percentage of respondents 0 10 20 30 40 50 60 70 80 90 100

Never | Several times a year | 1-3 times a month | Once a week | Several times a week | Daily

Turning from individual expressions to activities involving others, we find a similar diversity. Four out of 10 Brethren say that, apart from Sunday school, they *never* engage in small group prayer or Bible study with individuals beyond their own family. On the other hand, 30 percent meet with such a group on at least a monthly basis. Brethren of 75 years ago had a longstanding tradition of daily family devotions, sometimes focusing upon a specific space or time referred to as "the family altar." Today, less than one member in 10 (8 percent) has daily devotions with family members, nearly half (45 percent) concede that this is something they *never* do, and 7 out of 10 members say that they have such devotions once a month or less.

While half of today's Brethren say that they speak about their faith at least once a month to people beyond their immediate family and church circles, they are slow to invite such people to church activities. Responses to the survey also indicate that Brethren are much more comfortable with "showing others what it means to follow Jesus" than with "trying to convert others to faith in Christ." A majority (57 percent) indicate that they do the former at least once a week, while only 10 percent do the latter as frequently. Any attempt to convert, of course, is a more assertive activity than simply modeling discipleship in one's daily walk. Even so, the fact that 40 percent of today's Brethren say that they *never* attempt to convert someone to faith in Christ, and that another 36 percent do so only a few times a year, attests to something less than evangelistic zeal. To the extent that Brethren do welcome others, they do it quietly. Their outreach shares more in common with the "quiet in the land" approach of 19th-century Anabaptists than with the zeal of their early Pietist forebears.

Faith commitments and priorities

Another window into the faith of Brethren is to ask about their personal faith commitments. Respondents to the Brethren Member Profile were asked to rate the personal importance of each of 16 commitments on a four-category scale ranging from "not at all important" to "very important." Most were rated as important to some extent, so the key distinction is to rate a particular commitment as "very important" as opposed to only "fairly important."

Table 5.1 on page 40 presents in descending order the percent of Brethren who view each commitment as "very important."

True to their Radical Pietist legacy of a Christ-centered, Spirit-filled faith, Brethren today place greatest priority upon following Jesus and avoiding sin, nurturing spirituality, and manifesting Christ's spirit of love toward others. These form an "upper tier" of shared commitments that most Brethren cherish.

TABLE 5.1

Percentage of Brethren who rate each item as "Very Important" among their
personal faith commitments

Faith commitment	Percentage
Avoiding sin	79
Following Jesus in daily life	78
Spiritual growth	77
Expressing Christian love in all my relationships	74
Praising and glorifying God	72
Building strong bonds of community in the church	63
Serving others within the church	63
Practicing the spiritual disciplines	63
Serving others outside the church	60
Adult baptism	60
Peacemaking and nonviolence	56
Evangelizing non-believers	43
Living a simple lifestyle	41
Nonconformity to the world	40
Promoting social justice in the world	39
Giving and receiving counsel from other members	36

A second tier, still important but more likely to be considered only "fairly important," includes specific commitments such as serving others, building up the church, practicing the spiritual disciplines, adult baptism, and peacemaking and nonviolence. Although a majority of Brethren still rate these as "very important," the smaller percentages suggest that they are considered secondary or derivative, rather than the heart of the faith. A third and final tier includes commitments that are considered "very important" by only a minority of Brethren. These are evangelizing non-believers, simplicity and nonconformity, promoting social justice, and giving and receiving counsel from other members. The fact that receiving counsel falls to the bottom of the list is one more indicator of the personal rather than collective nature of the Brethren moral outlook at the outset of their fourth century. When members embrace a view that the conscience of the individual is the final arbiter in matters of daily living, then giving and receiving "admonitions," as the Brethren used to call them, no longer makes sense.

If praising God, following Jesus, growing spiritually, and avoiding sin are the essential Brethren faith commitments, what are the different streams that flow from this essence? The answer is complicated. The first thing to note is that some commitments are more pietistically tinged while others are more inherently relational. The former highlight the commandment to "Love the Lord your God with all your heart and with all your soul" and the longing for spiritual growth and purity. The latter highlight the commandment to "Love your neighbor as yourself," expressing faith by letting it ripple outward in relationships—"doing it unto the least of these, my brethren." As much as Brethren might want to hold these two streams (the impulses toward sanctification and benevolence) in balance, individual members often elevate one above the other, if for no reason other than that one involves less struggle for them personally.

When the impulse toward "spiritual growth" is stronger than "following Jesus in daily life," for instance, the balance can shift in one direction. When it shifts far enough, the interest in spiritual growth can generate a preoccupation with personal righteousness and a goal of avoiding sin *and* sinners. Such a preoccupation can sequester believers into a narrow faith-world conceived as a righteous enclave. From this moral pedestal, the most important actions toward outsiders become evangelism, baptizing them into the church, improving them, and preserving the church's purity. Beyond that, the social and relational implications of faith are conceived rather narrowly, in terms of nurturing and serving others within the church.

When the commitment to "follow Jesus in daily life," on the other hand, is stronger than "spiritual growth," the balance can similarly shift. In the extreme, social benevolence and human connection overshadow personal spirituality to such an extent that "expressing Christian love in all my relationships" becomes not a reflection of faith, but the essence of it. Following Jesus doesn't express personal piety, but supplants it. Such humanistically oriented Christians can even come to disdain more evangelical faith expressions. When this occurs, attempts to evangelize are disparaged as unloving activities that look down upon others, rather than lifting them up in Christian love. From this moral pedestal, the church is but an agent of service and social transformation. Peacemaking and nonviolence, promoting social justice, serving others outside the church, and building strong bonds of community within the church are enshrined as cardinal commitments. From this faith perspective, personal piety and evangelism seem somehow small.

These two streams, of course, are not generally this far out of balance. More typically the shift in faith commitments is subtle, with both spirituality and "good works" retaining a clear focus. This is seen in Brethren responses to the question "In your view, does salvation depend more on what a person believes or on how a person lives?" (see figure 5.2). Given the option to say "both," 60 percent of Brethren say that salvation "depends equally upon one's beliefs and how one lives."

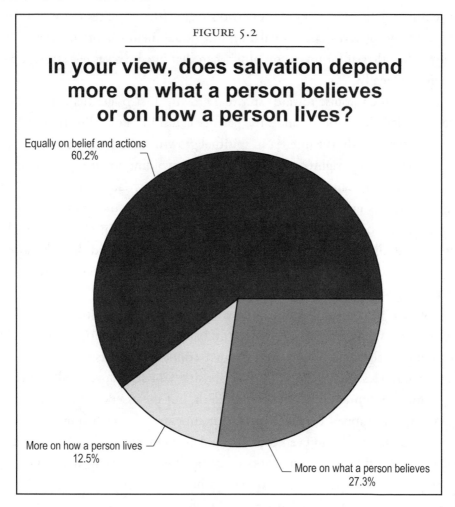

FIGURE 5.2

In your view, does salvation depend more on what a person believes or on how a person lives?

Equally on belief and actions
60.2%

More on how a person lives
12.5%

More on what a person believes
27.3%

This, however, does not suggest that the faith commitments of Brethren never diverge, that different streams of emphasis do not exist. Take the commitment to peace and nonviolence. Brethren have always believed that peace is a natural extension of faith because Christ fills Christians with a spirit of love that permeates all of their relationships. The commitment to peace was thus considered a direct outcome of the core commitments to glorify God, follow Jesus, and avoid sin. So, a question about the relative importance of peacemaking on the one hand and the spiritual disciplines (prayer, Bible study, and the like) on the other would have led early Brethren to question how you could have one without the other. Similarly, the Brethren Member Profile reveals that most Brethren today rate peacemaking and the spiritual disciplines as equally important (see figure 5.3). This is shown graphically in the pie chart on the left. The chart on the right shows the relative importance assigned to peacemaking versus evangelism.

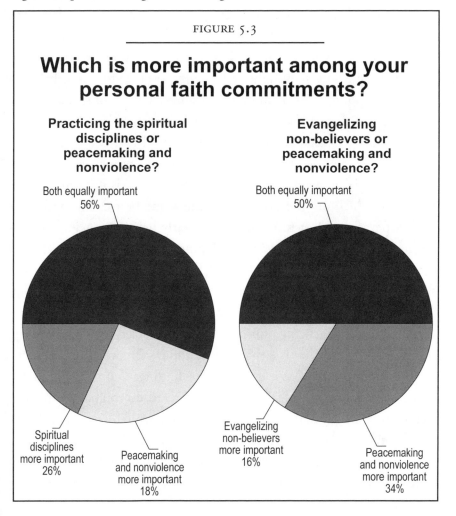

FIGURE 5.3

Which is more important among your personal faith commitments?

Practicing the spiritual disciplines or peacemaking and nonviolence?

Both equally important
56%

Spiritual disciplines more important
26%

Peacemaking and nonviolence more important
18%

Evangelizing non-believers or peacemaking and nonviolence?

Both equally important
50%

Evangelizing non-believers more important
16%

Peacemaking and nonviolence more important
34%

These relative faith priorities—these hierarchies of commitment—relate to Brethren theological positions in interesting ways. Consider, for instance, the differences in christology among the Brethren sub-groups defined by the pie on the right. Nearly 90 percent of those who say evangelizing is a more important personal commitment than peacemaking also say that "Jesus is the only way to God and those without faith in Jesus will not be saved." In contrast, those who view peacemaking as more important than evangelizing are less than half as likely to see Jesus as "the only way." A majority (62 percent) of the latter, in fact, believe that God will save people who don't know Jesus, and nearly 30 percent say either that "Jesus is one of many ways to God," or that "Jesus was a great teacher and prophet, but not more than that." Similar differences are evident in beliefs about Jesus' second coming. Sixty percent of Brethren who elevate evangelizing over peacemaking "eagerly anticipate Jesus' return to earth," compared to only 19 percent of those who elevate peacemaking over evangelizing. Also, 88 percent of those who assign higher relative importance to evangelizing say they would respond, "Yes, I know that I am saved" if someone inquired about their salvation status, compared to less than half (41 percent) of those who elevate peacemaking over evangelism. The other 59 percent of the latter group say one of the following: "I can't say for sure; only God knows whether I am saved" (40 percent), "being saved is not central to my faith" (15 percent), or "the people who know me best can answer better than I" (4 percent). Most fundamentally, nearly half (48 percent) of those who prioritize evangelism above peacemaking tend to believe that salvation depends more on what one believes than how one lives, while only 16 percent of those who attach greater importance to peacemaking say the same.

In the spectrum of personal faith commitments, it is noteworthy how far down the list evangelizing non-believers falls. In fact, it would be tempting to dismiss the fact that less than half of today's Brethren rate this activity as "very important" were it not for other findings that corroborate it.

When asked, for example, "How much interest do you have in planting new churches?" nearly half of the national membership (45 percent) say flat out that they are "not interested." Another 39 percent say that they favor church planting, but can do nothing more than contribute money. Only 16 percent say that they would be willing to become involved in any way other than finances. And even though 47 percent of the membership say that the Brethren should place more emphasis on evangelism than they do currently, this leaves slightly more than half who say the emphasis should not be any greater than at present.

All of this suggests that what at first blush might have seemed like a strong Brethren consensus on faith commitments is actually much more variegated.

Chapter 6 | **Church ordinances and worship**

Love feast

If we then begin in the footsteps of the Lord Jesus to live according to his commandment, then we can also hold communion together according to the commandment of Christ and his apostles in the fear of the Lord.[1]

Before the Brethren built meetinghouses for worship, they began to construct "love feast houses" to accommodate the larger numbers that gathered from a distance for communion. Brethren weren't the only Christians to celebrate a "love feast"—the Methodists, Moravians, and other groups of Pietist origin did so as well. But the Brethren did develop a unique formulation: a threefold service combining feetwashing with a full eschatological meal and a celebration of the eucharist. Together, these constituted a complete reenactment of Jesus' last supper with his disciples. But more than a reenactment, Brethren understood the love feast to be a direct response to Christ's commandment that they should "go and do likewise." Until the 1950s, the full love feast was the only communion celebration permitted for Brethren congregations; "bread and cup communion" was considered not only incomplete, but also a service that demanded less of the participant, and was therefore watered down. The historical practice was also to restrict participation to Brethren members "in good standing." While they might make room at the table for others to eat the full meal (the "Lord's Supper"), the eucharist was more restricted, lest someone should "eat or drink unworthily."

By the 1960s, most congregations had made room for alternate celebrations. Since that time, congregations have increasingly alternated Sunday morning "bread and cup communion" with the full love feast, experimented with alternate seating arrangements and menus for the love feast, and even made provisions for "hand washing" for members who have physical difficulty stooping to wash someone's feet. While some congregations continue to hold traditional love feasts in which the sexes are segregated at different tables, candles provide the only light, and conversation is kept to a minimum, it is increasingly evident that what is traditional varies from congregation to congregation. Even so, traditional fare at the meal generally consists of some kind of beef or lamb in a sandwich, the broth or "sop" created from cooking the meat, and sometimes fruit or cheese. Many variations on this basic theme occur, but the common element in "traditional" is that the meal is simple and unadorned, with minimal changes from service to service.

Even though love feast today isn't the climax of Brethren liturgical life that it once was, the majority of Brethren do attend. About two-thirds of the national membership (65 percent) say that they attend love feast at least once a year, a number that has not dropped during the last two decades. And the number of members nationally who say they have not attended during the past five years is lower, if anything, than 20 years ago. Only 23 percent of today's Brethren, less than a quarter of the membership, say that they haven't attended love feast in the last five years.

An interesting shift during the last two decades is in Pennsylvania. In 1985, I wrote that 77 percent of Pennsylvania Brethren attended love feast at least once a year, with two-thirds (67 percent) attending twice a year. At that time, rates of attendance in Pennsylvania clearly outpaced rates in other eastern and midwestern states. This is no longer the case. While Pennsylvania Brethren are still more likely to attend twice a year than members in other states, the number who do so has dropped from 67 percent to 53 percent. Similarly, the number of Pennsylvania Brethren who attend at least once a year has dropped from 77 percent to 71 percent, a figure that is virtually the same as in Virginia and West Virginia, and little different from attendance rates in Indiana or Illinois. While love feast attendance in Pennsylvania has slipped somewhat, putting it more on a par with other states, rates in Virginia and Indiana seem to have nudged upward.

Another noteworthy point is the reality of congregational variation. In every region of the country, love feast attendance is higher in some congregations than in others. Four-fifths of the Brethren Member Profile congregations have a majority reporting that they attend at least once a year. Even so, at 15 of the 128 congregations in our sample, the most common response to the question "How often have you attended the love feast in the past five years?" was *never*. Thankfully, this is not a large percentage of congregations. And the fact that these congregations are scattered geographically leads to

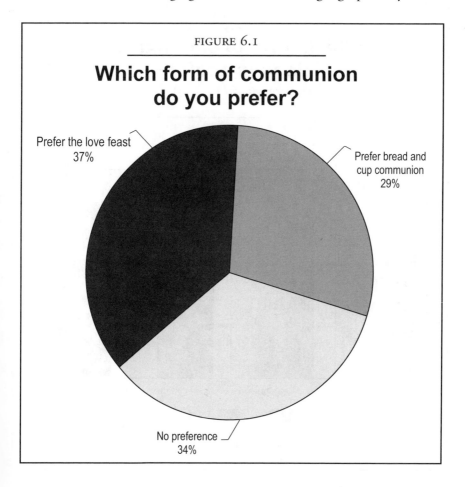

FIGURE 6.1

Which form of communion do you prefer?

Prefer the love feast
37%

Prefer bread and
cup communion
29%

No preference
34%

the conclusion that it has more to do with congregational variation itself than with location or region of the country.

Given the role of the love feast historically in the Church of the Brethren, and the fact that it was the only communion service officially permitted by Annual Conference until 1958, it is somewhat surprising that only a minority of today's Brethren express a preference for the love feast over "bread and cup" communion during worship. When asked which form of communion they prefer, Brethren nationwide respond as depicted in figure 6.1 (page 49).

Even though fewer than 4 of every 10 Brethren nationally report a preference for the love feast, there are groups with a stronger preference. Older Brethren, for example, have a much higher preference for the love feast than do younger Brethren. As a matter of fact, the clearly declining preference

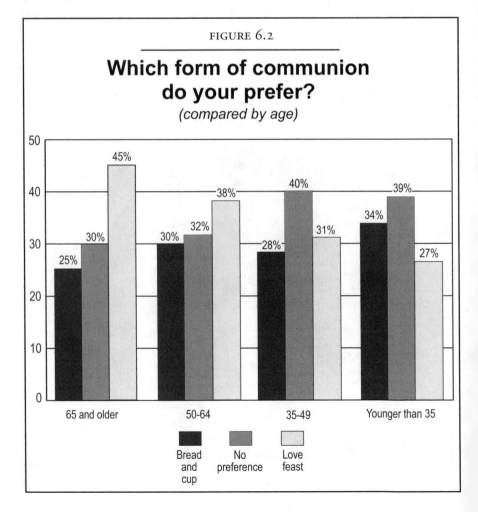

FIGURE 6.2

Which form of communion do your prefer?

(compared by age)

for love feast among younger age groups could mean one of two things: that younger Brethren are less inclined to speak in terms of a communion preference, or that it is only their preference for the love feast itself that has declined. The bar chart in figure 6.2 suggests that it is the latter rather than the former. While younger Brethren are more inclined to express "no preference," among those who do express a preference, younger Brethren are much more likely to express a preference for "bread and cup communion" than their parents and grandparents.

Shifts in sentiment and perception accompany this shift in preference. Brethren under age 35, for example, are nearly three times more likely to say that feetwashing is "awkward and uncomfortable" than are Brethren 65 and older. They are also less likely to feel that feetwashing is "spiritually moving and very meaningful." Interestingly, though, it is the younger Brethren who are most inclined to say that feetwashing "builds a deep sense of church community." Even as these feelings and perceptions of feetwashing vary by age, one thing remains constant: Hardly anyone—not even the young—says that feetwashing is "an outdated service that should fade away." Only about 7 percent of Brethren, regardless of age, believe it should be dispensed with altogether.[2]

A century ago, Brethren were still publishing tracts about *close communion,* contending that communion should be restricted not just to members, but only to members in good standing—those who weren't being disciplined for some offense against the church. In 1944, however, the concept of a "member in good standing" was finally dispensed with, because Brethren no longer drew disciplinary boundaries. What had once been perceived as a matter for church correction had come to be seen as a private, individual concern. Some congregations, especially in Pennsylvania, continued to "set members back" from communion for a failure to live up to church standards, but the practice had been abandoned throughout much of the denomination. In 1951, love feast participation was opened up to members of any Christian denomination.

And now, according to the 2006 Brethren Member Profile, church membership itself, regardless of denomination, no longer matters as a condition for participating in the love feast. When asked "who should be allowed to participate in the communion service during love feast?" only 18 percent, fewer than one of every five Brethren, mentioned church membership (in any church) as condition for participation. In contrast, over half (55 percent) said "anyone who accepts Jesus as Savior and Lord" should be allowed, and another 26 percent said that "anyone who wishes to" should be able to participate. The old Dunker concern that individuals should not partake "unworthily" has faded, along with traditional understandings of church purity. Most Brethren are happy to welcome anyone with an expressed faith in Christ to the table, and a substantial minority would not require that much.

Baptism

How can the poor Brethren help it that it is such an unusual performance, and that the true baptism of repentant sinners commanded by Jesus has become so strange and obscure that even the chosen ones are almost offended and repelled by it?[3]

During the 19th century, the pages that Brethren authors devoted to various "defenses" of baptism likely outnumbered the pages devoted to all other topics combined. Among the baptismal topics that were debated between 1850 and 1900 were whether new members had to be rebaptized if their prior baptisms had not been conducted in order (meaning with the appropriate questions and promises, in an appropriate setting, and with a properly Brethren type of dunking); whether baptisms could be conducted in a tub or pool rather than a stream; and what types of behavior—termed "tests of membership"—were required of those who wanted to join the church. During the late 19th century, even baptisms that were "in order" in every detail were ruled unacceptable if they hadn't been performed by a currently recognized German Baptist Brethren minister.

Earlier in the 19th century, there had been greater flexibility, but as the church grew and expanded geographically, Brethren established a specific "baptismal formula" in order to ensure a unity of practice. The 1848 baptismal formula included (1) an examination of the applicant by two or more ministers to discern the seriousness of their desire to join the church; (2) a requirement that the candidates promise, as members of the church, to refrain from conformity to the world, from any type of oath, and from the use of violence against humans; (3) a condition that the candidate promise to "hear the church" as laid out in Matthew 18; and (4) a confession of faith in Jesus, renunciation o

Satan and the sinful pleasures of the world, and promise of faithfulness until death. This baptismal formula was accepted as the standard from the time it was first issued until it began to fall into disuse during the 1920s and 1930s. Prior to each love feast, every member of the church was visited by deacons to ascertain whether they were living up to their baptismal promises. Since the establishment of the professional pastorate, however, and especially since the end of World War II, the behavioral standards earlier associated with baptism have been dropped. What remains is the confession of faith, and a generalized hope, not an expectation, that Brethren will simply do good.

In 1915 the requirement that everyone coming into the church had to be rebaptized was softened a bit, and in 1958 it was dispensed with altogether. From that point on, new members could be accepted from any other Christian denomination on a simple confession of faith, without being rebaptized by the Brethren. Today, most people who come to the Church of the Brethren from another denomination are not rebaptized, although a few choose adult baptism, believing that their prior infant baptism was insufficient or that they would simply like something more.

The Brethren Member Profile reveals that nearly 7 of every 10 members of today's Church of the Brethren (69 percent) were first baptized in a Brethren congregation. Interestingly, the typical age of baptism appears to have changed little since the 1930s. From young adults to senior citizens, most of today's Brethren were baptized between the ages of 11 and 17. If what is termed adult baptism is actually being offered to children and teens, as these data confirm, it has been that way for at least the last 60 or 70 years. By all indications, most of today's Brethren consider 11 or 12 to be the age of accountability where faith decisions are concerned.

Fully 87 percent of today's Brethren say that the idea of adult (rather than infant) baptism is important to them, with 60 percent saying it is *very* important. Yet 12 percent believe that "the Church of the Brethren should make some provision for baptizing infants," and another quarter are neutral about the desirability of infant baptism. When the response to both questions is considered together, it is clear that the adult baptism standard remains important to about two-thirds of today's Brethren.[4] Even so, when asked whether there is "any important way that the Church of the Brethren seems different to you from other Protestant denominations such as the Methodists or Presbyterians," both of which generally baptize infants, only 6 percent of today's Brethren think to mention baptism as an important difference. Even a cursory examination of historic church documents suggests that Alexander Mack and the early Brethren would have responded differently.

Worship

Not long after their early 18th-century emigrations to America, Brethren worship was described by one observer as involving such a clamor that one might wonder whether "their God were hard of hearing." At their centennial, in 1808, most Brethren still met for worship in homes rather than in meetinghouses. By this time, their language transition from English to German was underway, and worship had settled into a quietistic routine consisting of extemporaneous "exhorting" by multiple, unpaid ministers; scripture reading; prayer with the congregation kneeling; slowly sung, unaccompanied hymns; and the avoidance of many trappings of "popular Christianity." Later in the century, the pulse of Protestant evangelicalism—with its pulpits, offerings, collections, steeples, Sunday schools, and up-tempo gospel music—greatly affected the Brethren, influencing their worship to the point where their 1908 bicentennial was celebrated with gospel music sung from the first Brethren hymnal to incorporate musical notation along with the verse. What we commonly view today as the old-style religion of four-part gospel hymns was new enough then that the pace and energy of the songs made conservative Brethren cringe. Ironically, they wondered how one could hear God amongst the clamor, but their younger generations demanded it.

During the 20th century, Brethren houses of worship were transformed from plain meetinghouses in which Brethren had worshiped "sideways" (facing the side wall with ministers seated at a table) to respectable buildings with steeples, raised pulpits, fellowship halls, Sunday school classrooms, and indoor "facilities." Brethren ministers were transformed from a body of self-trained, unpaid men in beards and plain garb, to a mixed-sex body of salaried professionals with some amount of seminary training. Meetinghouses became "churches" in popular parlance, even though Brethren ministers continued to remind members that believers were actually the church. Stained glass divided chancels, indoor baptistries, organs, choirs, robes, and many other elements of religious finery were introduced. Specialized liturgical terminology—chancels, acolytes, Epiphany, eucharist, and many more—introduced Brethren to the forms and ways of larger Protestantism, which was now considered (by most) their religious home.

Whatever its form or flavor, corporate worship remains central to the Church of the Brethren. Seventy-one percent of today's Brethren report that they attend worship on a weekly basis. Half (51 percent) say that they attend Sunday school at least a couple of times a month. And nearly half (47 percent) spend more than an hour a week in congregational activities *beyond* worship services. While these figures accurately summarize the *reported behavior of our sample*, they should be met with a certain skepticism for two reasons: (1) survey respondents typically overstate their conformity to socially desirable norms, even in an anonymous survey; and (2) those who responded to the survey are likely to be more involved in congregational life than the one-third of sampled members who didn't respond.[5] Nonetheless, even in the face of declining membership nationally, Brethren investment in local congregational life remains high and seems fairly stable.[6]

Having migrated into the religious mainstream, it is not surprising that the debates and controversies of contemporary Christianity have become the debates and controversies of the Brethren. The style of Brethren worship, which was never completely stationary, has experienced a period of ferment and experimentation during the past 15 years after a half century of relative stability. During this time, worship styles have been subject to much critical examination. When handled sensitively, such scrutiny can actually build up the body of the church by making worship more meaningful. But critical examination can also cause a disturbance. Where diverse religious expressions coexist among the members of a single congregation, each expression can feel like home to some, yet alien to others. Brethren congregations attempt to accommodate this diversity in different ways. Some retain a single service, but vary their worship from week to week. Others attempt to blend diverse elements (that do not always easily coexist) within a single service. Others hold multiple services, calling one contemporary or informal to contrast it with another that is more traditional or formal. Other congregations have been little touched by the dilemma, in some cases because they have few young members, and in others because they are more isolated, or because they do a better job involving young adults in traditional services as worship and music leaders. Within 50 miles of my home in Augusta County, Virginia, there are Brethren congregations that fit into each of these categories.

In Brethren cultural geography, Virginia's Shenandoah Valley is understood to occupy a conservative niche socially, politically, and religiously. And yet the ease and frequency with which they address God in worship as "Father God" is more typical of the entire denomination than one might suspect. Even though the latest Brethren hymnal made efforts to temper exclusively masculine images of God, the Brethren Member Profile reveals that referring to God as "Father" or "He" remains the overwhelming preference of the majority of today's Brethren (see figure 6.3). Three-quarters of the membership feel positively about masculine terminology for God, compared to only 6 percent who feel negative. By contrast, only 6 percent of today's Brethren say they feel positively about references to God as "Mother" or "She" compared to 77 percent who feel negatively. No other question about worship generates such a strong consensus.

In addition to the "Father God" preference, Brethren express a clear preference for a number of other traditional worship forms. Organ music, litanies and responsive readings, altar calls, personal faith testimonies, and hymns with four-part harmony are all widely favored as regular parts of worship. Contemporary praise songs and the applauding of singers or musicians are also viewed positively by a majority of Brethren. Technological innovations, on the other hand, such as projecting images on a large screen or using electric guitars and drums, are favored by only a minority. Brethren are most reticent, though, about spiritual gestures such as dance, raising hands in praise, and especially people praying aloud while the minister prays.

Since 1990, some Brethren congregations have expanded their worship repertoire by adding a "contemporary" service. Typically, this service is more expressive and informal than the worship style typical of the mid-20th century. In some cases the contemporary service replaces the conventional service, while in others the conventional service is an early service, before the "main" service.

It would be a mistake, however, to surmise that the worship preferences of today's Brethren are as neatly classified into conventional or contemporary

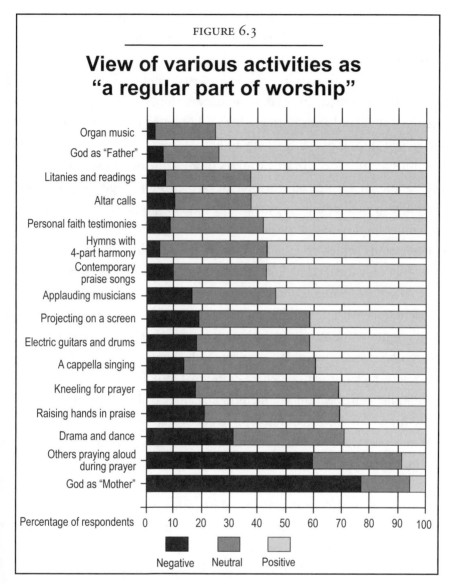

FIGURE 6.3

View of various activities as "a regular part of worship"

Organ music
God as "Father"
Litanies and readings
Altar calls
Personal faith testimonies
Hymns with 4-part harmony
Contemporary praise songs
Applauding musicians
Projecting on a screen
Electric guitars and drums
A cappella singing
Kneeling for prayer
Raising hands in praise
Drama and dance
Others praying aloud during prayer
God as "Mother"

Percentage of respondents   0   10   20   30   40   50   60   70   80   90   100

Negative   Neutral   Positive

categories as the services themselves. The truth is that some prefer conventional forms: organ music, litanies and readings, and hymns with four-part harmony. Some prefer innovations: contemporary praise songs, electric guitars and drums, projecting onto a large screen, and drama and dance. And many are happy with a mix of the two. For example, two-thirds of those who feel positive about contemporary praise songs also feel positive about hymns with four-part harmony. And those who are neutral about one are likely to be neutral about the other. So support for traditional and contemporary forms should probably be gauged independently, like temperature and barometric pressure, rather than being viewed as opposite ends of a single spectrum.

And regarding worship, there is at least one other factor that operates independently: the emotionality of worship, especially when visible emotional displays are concerned. In a contemporary setting, such displays might include the waving of hands during a hymn, holding hands aloft or with palms outstretched during prayer, praying audibly—"yes, Lord," "praise you Jesus," etc.—during a minister's prayer, or tears of joy at being in God's presence. In more traditional settings, spiritual fervor or contrition might be expressed by responding to an altar call, or by shouting "Amen" in response to the minister. Both contemporary and traditional services may offer a time for testimonies and confessions, which are usually emotionally laden because of their personal nature. Not only the level of emotion but also the kind of emotion varies from service to service. Some "contemporary" services, for example, are exuberant and celebratory with dancing and guitars, while others are more hushed and beatific. Some emotions are displayed more effervescently, and some, more serenely. Quiet reverence itself, even when indistinguishable from daydreaming to an observer, can be considered an emotional response. So a description of a still and quiet congregation as "unemotional" may be far off the mark.

Brethren who share a common preference for more conventional religious forms may part ways over the amount of emotional expression they desire in worship. Some prefer an attitude of quiet listening, while others prefer a more active outpouring of love, concern, and support. And those who share a penchant for worship innovation may part company over whether the service is primarily an innovative performance or one inviting praise and personal involvement from all of the participants. In a word, between tradition, innovation, and emotion, all of which vary independently to at least a degree, today's Brethren come in many varieties with many distinct combinations of worship preference. Minimally, we should think at least in terms of four different worship styles.

Contemporary worship preferences come in at least two varieties: a *praise preference* that finds meaning in visible expression; and a *performance preference* that shifts the focus away from one's own spiritual state toward various forms of musical and liturgical innovation. The praise preference center worship in the emotional response of the worshipers, while the performanc preference centers worship upon the "stage," celebrating diversity and innovation as long as it requires little personal disclosure from those attending. The praise preference rejects organ music as too formal and overpowering, while the performance preference includes the organ among a retinue of instruments that help to diversify the production. Formal litanies and responsive readings are too structured and constrained to freely express the praise preference, but are welcomed by the performance preference because they reflect corporate sentiment more than personal emotion. Based upon the Brethren Member Profile, my best estimate is that about 37 percent of today's Brethren have a preference for contemporary praise services, while fewer than half that number, about 15 percent, prefer an innovative performance that draws attention away from their own spiritual state.

Traditional worship preferences also come in at least two varieties: a *confessional preference*, which welcomes emotional display as long as it is expressed in traditional ways (altar calls, faith testimonies, and hymn singing, without the intrusion of guitars, drums, and large screens); and a *conventional preference*, which seeks a more formulaic worship consisting of four-part hymns, litanies and readings, thoughtful sermons, and carefully prepared musical numbers. While both the confessional and the conventional preference are traditional in the sense that they are more oriented toward a worship continuity than toward liturgical trailblazing, they differ—like their contemporary praise and performance counterparts—in the desirability of visible displays of emotion. Personal emotional disclosure is welcomed by the confessional preference, while it is at best endured by the conventional preference. The confessional preference gravitates toward a more informal, "low church," extemporaneous worship experience, while the conventional preference gravitates toward a more carefully scripted, liturgical style of worship. Congregations with Bethany Seminary-trained pastors tended toward what I am calling "conventional" between the 1940s and 1980s, while those with ministers from more evangelical backgrounds (Southern Baptist, for instance) likely evidenced a more confessional style of traditional worship. My best estimate is that about 16 percent of today's Brethren have a preference for traditional, confessional services, while twice as many (32 percent) prefer a less emotional traditional service, which I have called conventional.

So all things considered, the Brethren faith family is about evenly divided today between those preferring traditional forms of worship and those preferring something more contemporary. The denomination is also equally divided between those who are comfortable with personal displays of feeling and those who prefer a more structured focus upon the front of the sanctuary. While the more scripted style of worship is the primary preference of those who favor traditional forms, the more emotional and spontaneous style predominates among those who gravitate toward the contemporary. Brethren younger than 35 express a marked preference for praise services, while Brethren of retirement age have nearly as strong a preference for conventional services (see figure 6.4).

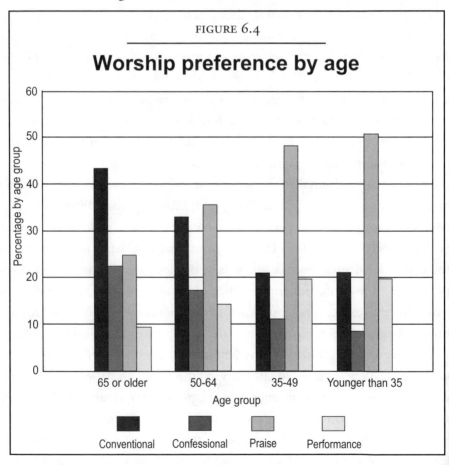

FIGURE 6.4

Worship preference by age

Peace and military service

So, we believe where that fire which Christ came to kindle burns, there will be burnt all war as predicted; for the love to God constrains to the obedience of his commandments. . . . We hope the dear brethren will not take it amiss when we can not see or find any liberty to use any (carnal) sword, but only the sword of the Spirit, which is the word of God.[1]

The early Brethren knew a secret: The core of the Christian peace witness was in the heart of the believer. In their view, true Christians refused to fight *not* out of a principled opposition to war or violence, but because they could not do otherwise. If the spirit of Christ had genuinely transformed their hearts, then their consciences invariably prevented acts of violence and aggression. They understood that their own will, on the other hand, reflecting their own self-interest, would lead toward a defense of self, as it did for Peter in the garden of Gethsemane. Joining the church, however, signaled the believer's willingness to let "conscience toward God" override their own opinions, molding them into a unity that, like the Amish in a recent schoolhouse shooting, returned good for evil, a witness to God's redemptive forgiveness. As Christians, early Brethren understood that their primary charge was to follow not a political or practical argument, but Jesus' example and teachings. When Jesus was reviled and personally threatened, they observed, he responded by suffering and praying for his enemies. Because Jesus' example is not the way of the world, and because the Brethren would always hear compelling rationales for military involvement, they were admonished to "exercise and associate with those that love peace, and pursue it." Their assurance was, "If you love peace and seek it yourself, the spirit of peace will be with you, and there will always be brethren that will be like-minded."[2]

Because of this view of the essence of Christian spiritual transformation, Brethren disciplined members who took up arms during the American War of Independence and the Civil War. Even the torching of their communities by Sheridan's armies wasn't sufficient motive to join neighbors in defending property and livelihood. The uncertainty associated with Brethren participation in World War I focused upon the wearing of the uniform by men serving the military in a noncombatant role, not whether it was acceptable for Brethren to fight, which wasn't even open for discussion.

Between the two World Wars of the past century, the issue of war and peace was repeatedly considered by the Brethren's Annual Meeting. The resulting statements were resolute in their portrayal of both the church's peace heritage and its contemporary witness to the world. These excerpts from the 1935 Annual Conference statement typified Brethren positions of the interwar period.

> As a people we have opposed wars at all times throughout our entire history of over two hundred twenty-five years and we have stood with equal consistency for constructive peace principles in all relationships of life. We hate war because we love peace, our way of life at all times. It has been the practice of the church through the years to require of applicants for membership a pledge not to engage in war nor learn the art of war. . . .

> We believe that all war is sin; that it is wrong for Christians to support or to engage in it; and that war is incompatible with the spirit, example and teachings of Jesus. We believe that war is not inevitable. Those beliefs are not based upon a peculiar peace doctrine of our own; they arise from our application of Christian standards to all human relations, whether individual, group, class, or national. To settle conflicts in any of these relationships by war is not efficient, not constructive, not permanent, and certainly not Christian. . . .

We believe the whole war system is futile, always leaving more prob-
lems than it settles, if it settles any. Today, only a few years after win-
ning the "war to end war," the United States is in the midst of the
greatest of war preparation, and our country shares with other nations
the general feeling of insecurity throughout the world. . . . [T]he fruit
of war is not democracy; war destroys democracy as the prevalence
of dictatorships of the communist, fascist, or other varieties, testifies.
We cannot "make the world safe for democracy" by war.[3]

The unrelenting message was this: (1) War always violates the spirit and teachings of Jesus; and (2) faith convictions should mold the conscience of Christians accordingly. Any participation in war was deemed "not Christian."

In spite of such resolve, the 1940s witnessed the vast majority of young
Brethren entering military service in support of a popular war. Prior to World
War II, Brethren still questioned whether church discipline would be en-
forced against members who violated the Brethren ban on military service.
By the 1940s, however, "tests of membership" were generally a thing of the
past, leaving Brethren free to follow their personal preferences with respect
to military service. By most accounts, the consciences of about 80 percent
of young Brethren permitted them to join the armed forces even though
the 1939 Annual Conference ruled that such men were not "in full accord"
with the church and that efforts should be made to bring them back into
full accord. It was evident, though, that Brethren soldiers would not be disciplined, a reality that was confirmed by a 1948 statement that articulated a
new Brethren doctrine of "individual conscience."

Inasmuch as the church believes in the right of individual conscience,
it recognizes that various positions on war and military service will be
taken by its members. . . . Some believe it to be their Christian obli-
gation to render full or limited military service. . . . The church seeks
to maintain a fellowship of all who sincerely follow the guidance of
conscience.[4]

The position that "all war is sin" was re-articulated in the same statement,
yet these words were increasingly received as abstract pronouncements rather
than as directives to Brethren members, leaving church leaders to wonder
how many were listening.

During the Vietnam conflict, Annual Conference reaffirmed its position that all war is sin and that Brethren "cannot, in the event of war, accept military service or support the military machine in any capacity." The entire church program of the Brethren was described as being designed to lead individuals into "such intimate contact with Jesus Christ, our Lord, that they will commit themselves to Him" and to a life of "love and nonviolence as a central principle of Christian conduct."[5] Twenty years later (in 1991), a new statement on peacemaking echoed these same teachings:

[W]hen called upon to participate in warfare, Brethren should heed the words of the New Testament and the example of Christ in refusing to take part in the destruction of human life. Instead, the church should teach the way of conscientious objection and support those who choose it. This is the way of Christ.

[C]ongregations are encouraged to . . . provide counseling for young men and women as they make career choices and as they face the possibility of military conscription, encouraging young people to serve as conscientious objectors during time of war in accordance with Brethren understandings of the New Testament. . . .

A faithful peace witness today on the part of the church will require biblical non-resistance, prophetic declarations, unpopular actions, peace service (standing with the oppressed and serving their need), and public policy advocacy.

[T]he Church of the Brethren . . . declares that peace is the will of God and all war is sin; calls all its members not to participate in the military in any way and to find constructive avenues of peacemaking; proclaims that our first allegiance is to God even when obedience requires civil disobedience; condemns the outrageous expenditures of the state for military forces and weapons of destruction, and condemns national security doctrines and strategies of deterrence that rationalize such expenditures and the militarization of societies; calls for complete nuclear, biological and chemical weapons disarmament. . . . [6]

The paper's conclusion? At the *"heart of Church of the Brethren life i* *a commitment both to live within God's peace and to be peacemakers."* On could not imagine a stronger series of statements reaffirming the Brethren peace legacy and witness to the world.

It is one thing, though, to adopt an official position at Annual Conference and quite another to actualize that position in the lives of church members. Yet if the members are indeed the *church*, it is sensible to question where the *actual* church position resides. Is it in official denominational statements or in the hearts of those who call themselves Brethren? If the latter, then the 2006 Brethren Member Profile offers a glimpse, albeit an imperfect one, of the Brethren peace position at the tricentennial of the Brethren movement. We can expect, of course, that the membership will fall short of the prophetic stand articulated by Annual Conference. The question is, How far short? And is there any similarity between official pronouncement and the reality of what Brethren do and think?

One issue that has a bearing upon this question is that of military participation: To what extent do today's Brethren consider it wrong to fight in a war? During the 1930s, as many as 60 percent of Brethren men agreed that it was "wrong to help in any war by fighting."[7] Twenty years ago, only 38 percent of Brethren (men and women) still agreed with this statement. Today, only 25 percent—one member in four—say it is wrong to fight in *any* war. Such softening of opposition to military combat is mirrored in members' views of how the church should instruct its youth. Even though the official position recommends that congregations counsel young men and women to become conscientious objectors during time of war, only 18 percent of today's Brethren—fewer than one in five—believe that young persons should be counseled against entering the military (see figure 7.1 on page 66). This is down from 26 percent during the 1980s, and has declined even further from the likely response of Brethren a decade or two earlier.[8] The youngest respondents in our tricentennial sample are those *least* likely to feel that Brethren youth should be counseled against military service. If Brethren still consider war a sin at all, they clearly believe that individual members are the best judges of whether it is "sinful" to sin. The church, in any event, should not counsel young people one way or the other.

Another interpretation of these responses is that Brethren have come to dissociate "military service" from "war," the latter being sinful, and the former generally acceptable. Only 21 percent of today's Brethren consider it

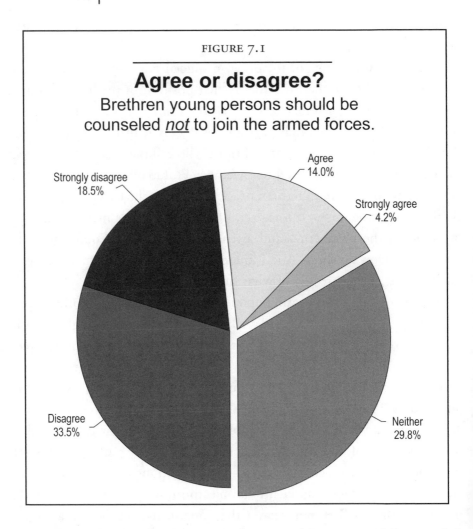

FIGURE 7.1

Agree or disagree?
Brethren young persons should be counseled _not_ to join the armed forces.

Agree
14.0%

Strongly agree
4.2%

Strongly disagree
18.5%

Neither
29.8%

Disagree
33.5%

"usually" or "always" wrong to enter the United States armed forces, while more than double that number (46 percent) say that it is "rarely" or "never" wrong. On a moral spectrum of "never-to-always wrong," Brethren classify military service as less objectionable than viewing pornography, buying an expensive sports car, copying a music CD, and using profanity (see figure 7.2). On their ledger of moral "don'ts," entering the military is about as wrong as taking prescription medications to reduce anxiety. If it is a vice at all, few are saying so.

Given these views, it is not surprising that Brethren views of the armed forces are more favorable than their heritage would suggest. Nearly three-quarters of today's Brethren (73 percent) believe the United States should

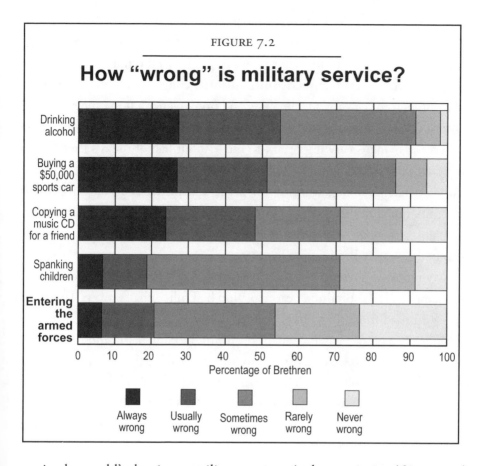

FIGURE 7.2

How "wrong" is military service?

Percentage of Brethren

Always wrong | Usually wrong | Sometimes wrong | Rarely wrong | Never wrong

Categories (top to bottom): Drinking alcohol, Buying a $50,000 sports car, Copying a music CD for a friend, Spanking children, **Entering the armed forces**

remain the world's dominant military power. A clear majority (61 percent) say that the U.S. armed forces "should continue the fight against terror until all serious threats have been eliminated," and a similar number (58 percent) view the War on Terror as a "religious battle between the forces of good and evil." The clear implication is that military enlistees are doing God's bidding in taking up arms to suppress the terrorist threat. During the spring of 2006, about half of today's Brethren (47 percent) said that the United States "did the right thing by going to war in Iraq." This is virtually identical to the number of Americans nationally who were saying the same thing.[9] Brethren attitudes toward the military are clearly not those of a dissenting religious minority; they reflect the diversity of the broader culture more than the unique heritage that earned the Brethren recognition as a "peace church."

Another component of the *actual* peace position is the Brethren view of the morality of war itself. Annual Conference statements notwithstanding, nearly half (44 percent) of the membership rejects the denominational position that "all war is sin." That said, it is significant that just over half (56 percent) remain persuaded, even though the majority of this group say it is not always wrong to fight in "sinful" wars. A similarly small majority clings to nonviolence as a core value: 56 percent classify peacemaking and nonviolence among their "very important" faith commitments, and 54 percent say that "complete nonviolence as a way of living is very important to me." About half of today's Brethren say that their pastors should make issues of peace and social justice a high priority, and 46 percent say that working for peace and justice is a "very important" denominational ministry of the Church of the Brethren. Clearly, peacemaking as an abstract ideal—an enduring hope grounded in Christian faith—is still treasured by many Brethren.

My repeated references to "about half of today's Brethren" raises the obvious question, Is the Brethren peace position half full, or half empty? Those who expect a broad moral consensus against violence—who have learned that the Brethren are a peace people—will be deeply disappointed, but those with more modest expectations may be pleased to find that half of the denomination still embraces a strong, albeit ill-defined commitment to peacemaking.

What is more, if we drop the bar far enough to include Brethren who *lightly* endorse Christian peace principles, we find that the cup is nearly full. About 9 of every 10 Brethren say that (1) peacemaking and nonviolence are at least "fairly important" personal commitments; (2) their pastor should give issues of peace and social justice at least a "medium" priority; and (3) the Church of the Brethren's ministry of peace and justice is at least "fairly important."[10] Many, of course, would rate nearly any respectable value as "fairly important" or as a "medium priority," so these numbers should not be trumpeted too loudly. Yet we can at least conclude that the 90 percent of Brethren who fall into this camp are not averse to the peace witness; it retains a certain resonance with them. Most Brethren understand that "peace" is a basic Christian principle, even though their views of how to practice, to live it, are vastly different.

This diversity of application is clearest when Brethren are asked, "Whether you are male or female, if you were 20 years old and faced with a military draft, what position would you take?" This was asked of adult church members regardless of their age, and the response is anything but united (see figures 7.3 and 7.4). At the Brethren tricentennial, nearly two-thirds of the membership

(63 percent) say they would choose military service, a position that Annual Conference has classified as everything from un-Christian to "not recommended" during the last 100 years (even though respect should be shown to those who adopt this view). The two-thirds who would enter the military are about

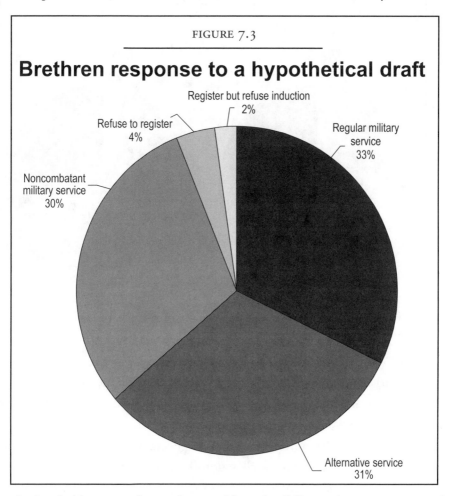

FIGURE 7.3

Brethren response to a hypothetical draft

Register but refuse induction
2%

Refuse to register
4%

Regular military
service
33%

Noncombatant
military service
30%

Alternative service
31%

evenly divided between those who would render full, combatant service and those who favor a noncombatant role. The remaining third of today's Brethren embrace one of the nonmilitary options recommended by Annual Conference, typically some form of alternative service, but with a few espousing positions of noncooperation.[11]

These responses to a hypothetical situation are directly related to the real decisions that family members have made vis-à-vis military service. In cases where no immediate family member has served, less than half of today's Brethren

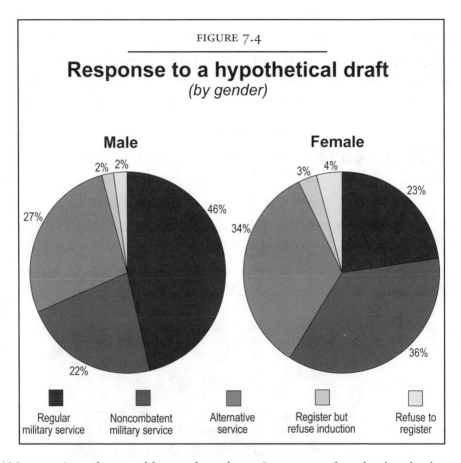

FIGURE 7.4

Response to a hypothetical draft
(by gender)

Male

2% 2%
27%
46%
34%
22%

Female

3% 4%
23%
36%

Regular military service | Noncombatent military service | Alternative service | Register but refuse induction | Refuse to register

(46 percent) say they would enter the military. In cases, on the other hand, where more than one family member has served, more than three-quarters (76 percent) say that they too would serve. Family traditions of service, whatever the type of service, are handed down from generation to generation. These traditions reproduce themselves in the daily conversations between parents and children, and then intersect with other family traditions to shape the normative climate of local congregations. Even though abundant individual exceptions can be noted, patterns of service tend to reproduce themselves by molding what seems normal or offensive, Christian or un-Christian, to members of the church.

Given this mixed peace portrait, it is no wonder that recent descriptions of the Church of the Brethren as a "living peace church" are laden with confession and qualification. A 2003 Annual Conference resolution confessed to many of the same peace shortcomings that we find in this survey, and yet the concluding section of the resolution ("We resolve to follow Jesus. . . .") focused more upon desirable *processes*—prayer, dialogue, confession, discovery, study, reporting, struggle, and seeking—than upon the practical substance of a Christian peace witness in a post-9/11 era. No clear action guidelines were offered.

Brethren clearly struggle with what it means to live "in peace and love" in an era when two-thirds (65 percent) of Brethren have immediate family members who have served in the armed forces. Most members support the military mobilization against international terrorism. Three-quarters believe that the United States should preserve its status as the world's dominant military power. Even in this militarized context, the 2006 Annual Conference managed to pass a resolution calling for a removal of troops from Iraq, but the vote was underwhelming. During the deliberations passionate voices spoke in favor of military intervention as well as against it. One thing that stood out in the debate was the nearly total lack of reference to the heritage—to historic Brethren understandings of war, military service, and violence in general. It was as if there were no heritage to draw upon, or as if the heritage carried so little weight that no one cared to invoke it. A "personal stories" and "emotional disclosure" approach to discussion was the discursive modality of the day.

Three hundred years ago, Alexander Mack wrote extensively about the corrosive impact of personal opinion and individual conscience upon genuine Christian witness. In his view and that of the early Brethren, to fail to rebuke sin under the pretense of "love" was to display a feigned or false love.

> This kind of love says: 'Leave me alone in my own will, opinion, and actions, and I will leave you alone in yours; we will love each other and be brethren. . . .' Unfortunately, we stayed long enough in this pernicious hypocritical love, while we were still among the Pietists. Now we have learned, and must continue to learn, that kind of love which hates and punishes wickedness and evil.[12]

Many have noted that the primary motivation for the first Brethren baptisms—the very organization of the movement—was a desire to more completely obey Christ's commandments. Mack denounced people who "become so confused in different ways that finally they do not know what they think or believe," suggesting that when they cannot accept what is clearly taught in scripture they simply manufacture their own faith and doctrine.

The consequence, he pointed out, was "complete disaster"—they "no longer believe in anything, but again fell victim to the world and the wide path."[13] It would be misleading in this age to call Mack a biblical literalist, yet he did believe that, if his brethren had Christ's spirit written into their hearts, they would willingly subject themselves to the letter of the New Testament. Those who did not, Mack wrote, wound up orienting themselves toward other, nonscriptural truths grounded in "haughty opinions."[14] I have to wonder how Mack, were he alive today, would characterize the peace witness of the Brethren reflected in the members of the church after 300 years.

During the past century, many have raised questions about the strength and direction of the Brethren peace witness. During the 1940s, Rufus Bowman, president of Bethany Seminary, wrote that "the statements which we so often hear today, 'Let your conscience be your guide,' 'Follow your conscience,' are not in harmony with our Brethren heritage. Our church fathers believed that there was a higher source of authority than individual opinions, conviction, and conscience."[15] During the 1950s, Floyd Mallott raised questions about the frailty of Brethren pacifism, noting that "the facts must not be hidden. The apathy of the pews is disconcerting."[16] Kermit Eby issued similar critiques and challenges regarding Brethren accommodation to mainstream American culture. From the 1960s through the current decade other Brethren leaders—Donald Durnbaugh and Dale Brown among them—have worried openly about a dearth of leadership and prophetic voice on issues of war and peace.

In his recent book *Another Way of Believing*, Brown takes comfort in the fact that Annual Conference positions (what he calls our "corporate" witness and I have called our "official" position) continue to take a strong prophetic stand against violence, war, and the things that make for war. Brown expresses hope that such statements reflect a surviving Christian spirit of peace among the Brethren, a spirit that will continue to mold both Annual Conference statements and the lives of individual Brethren. In fact, Brown's hope for the future of the Brethren focuses squarely upon their peace legacy: "For our future, I am proposing we focus on being a peace church. This choice or passion need not be the only thing we are about, but it could highlight who we are as Brethren."[17]

For such aspirations to be realized, however, the peace standoff revealed by the Brethren Member Profile will have to be addressed. The trend of the last 50 years, at least at the level of the membership, has been away from the focus Brown desires. The tipping of Brethren history away from a clear classification of certain behaviors as violations of the New Testament, and toward an ethic of dialogue with other Brethren (whatever their convictions might be), has left the Brethren in a spot where it is difficult for them to speak prophetically *as a church* to other traditions and communities.

Brethren individuals of course still draw upon their heritage to challenge the broader culture. Even so, the *actual* Brethren peace position (as I have called it) seems closer to Jimmy Carter's recent admission that "I never felt that my dedication to military service was a violation of my faith in Jesus Christ, the Prince of Peace" than to the official Brethren position that all war is sin and that Brethren should not support it in any way.[18] To be sure, there are still Brethren ministers who preach openly that they can't personally understand how one can claim to be a Christian without being a pacifist. But there are many others who openly support American military actions, and even district leaders who consider the Brethren peace position to be part of a broader liberal agenda that they want no part of.

Chapter 8 | The 'moral issues'

Whether we like it or not, the broader culture has classified a limited set of social concerns as the "moral issues" of our time. Even though some have struggled to broaden this understanding and others to shift it, most Americans continue to think of abortion and homosexuality as critical moral issues of our day. Other issues such as pornography, promiscuity, stem cell research, euthanasia, divorce, drugs, and alcohol are frequently added to the list, often lumped together under the banner of "conservative" or "family" values. Many Christians can agree that all of these are morally problematic at some level. But abortion and homosexuality, especially gay marriage, have become the battleground issues that set a litmus test of Christian faithfulness for many Americans.

Historically, Brethren have believed in sacred restraint where many of these vices are concerned. During the 1930s, for example, public confessions were often required from female members who had their babies "too early." Prior to the 1940s, Brethren were disciplined for a variety of sexual and alcohol-related offenses. During the early 1960s, many ministers still refused to re-marry divorced members. In 1993, conservative members mobilized to seek the resignation of an Annual Conference moderator for being too liberal on homosexuality. Annual Conference position papers continue to witness against many of these personal issues, often by blending earnest efforts to delineate the Christian lifestyle with respect for individual conscience and calls for ministry to those with personal struggles.

To assess Brethren views of "personal morality," the Brethren Member Profile used an approach common in survey research. Brethren were asked to rate a list of 26 behaviors on a scale from "never wrong" to "always wrong," the goal being to establish a hierarchy of moral concerns. The set of behaviors is limited, to be sure, and omits broader issues pertaining to economic justice, environmental protection, and the like, but it does offer a glimpse of the personal behaviors that Brethren find morally offensive. Of the 26 items on the list, five in particular stand out as objectionable to Brethren: extramarital sex, smoking marijuana, viewing pornographic materials, watching adult movies, and homosexual relations between consenting adults (see figure 8.1). A large majority of the membership consider all of these to be "always wrong." Less offensive, but still considered by most to be always wrong, are smoking cigarettes, cursing, lying, and premarital sex. Surprisingly, abortion—generally considered a pivotal moral controversy—is rated as more often acceptable than smoking cigarettes or telling a lie. This pertains only to how *often* abortion is considered acceptable though, not to the moral gravity of the offense. Cursing, for example, even though considered "always wrong" by a larger number of Brethren, is likely viewed as a lighter-weight transgression than abortion.

Interestingly, divorce and alcohol, two offenses with a long Annual Conference history, receive mixed reviews among today's Brethren. A century ago, both were Brethren moral benchmarks. Alcohol established a boundary between "Brethren in good standing" and others like Catholics and Episcopalians, whom Dunkers suspected were drunkards. Divorce, on the other hand, distinguished "good Christians" from those who for one reason or another fell short. Brethren were routinely the subjects of church discipline for transgressing either of these lines. Today, fewer than one member in 10 insists that divorce is "always wrong." Only four in 10—still a minority—believe that it is even "usually" wrong. A slight majority, on the other hand, still believe that consuming alcohol is usually wrong, with the remainder saying that it is only sometimes wrong, if that. This suggests that about half of the denomination still thinks in terms of the immorality of alcohol *per se*, while the other half focuses more upon overindulgence.

These moral assessments vary considerably by generation. Eight out of 10 elderly Brethren (79 percent), for example, say that alcohol is usually or always wrong, compared to only 28 percent of young Brethren.[1] These

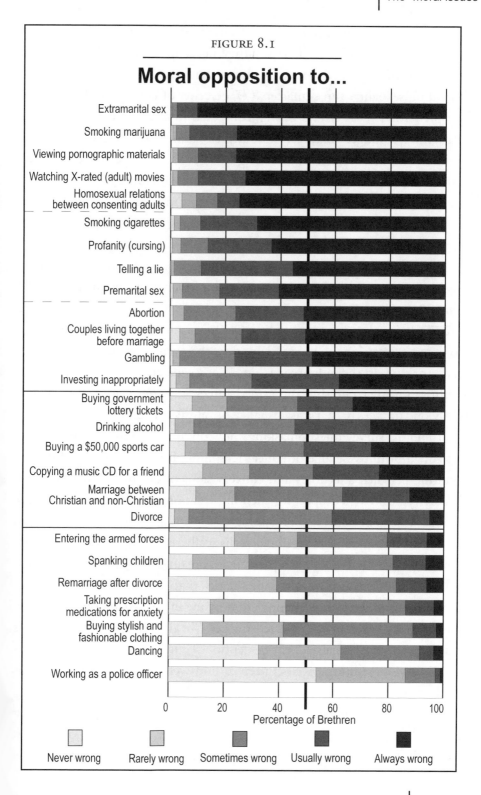

FIGURE 8.1

Moral opposition to...

Percentage of Brethren

Never wrong | Rarely wrong | Sometimes wrong | Usually wrong | Always wrong

ethical assessments correspond closely to their actual behavior. Three-quarters of the older group (76 percent) say they never drink alcohol, while three-quarters of the younger group (74 percent) admit that they sometimes do. Regarding sexuality, three-quarters (77 percent) of elderly Brethren believe that premarital sex is always wrong, compared to less than half (49 percent) of Brethren younger than 40. Similarly two-thirds (65 percent) of elderly Brethren say that it is always wrong for couples to live together before marriage, compared to only 37 percent of young Brethren.

The 26 behaviors that Brethren were asked to assess include some that are now considered generally acceptable. Working as a police officer, for instance, once classified as off limits for Brethren, is now accepted by virtually the entire denomination. Similarly, dancing, which raised eyebrows as late as the 1960s, is considered "usually wrong" by fewer than one member in 10. Remarriage after divorce, which once received stronger sanctions than divorce itself, is now accepted with little question. And finally, rejecting Annual Conference assertions that "we cannot, in the event of war, accept military service or support the military machine in any capacity," nearly half of today's Brethren say that entering the armed forces is "rarely" or "never" wrong. (Only one in five say that it is "usually" or "always" wrong.)

Though a survey question asking "how often" something is wrong is admittedly a primitive gauge of ethical reasoning, it does offer something beyond the personal anecdotes and conversations of our own social networks that are typically relied upon for such information. What is more, when the response rate to a scientific survey is high, as it was in this case, we gain a high level of confidence that the findings realistically reflect the conscious perceptions of the national membership. After all, the questionnaires are completed alone and anonymously, minimizing the risk that those who take the time to respond are trying to "be anything" for anyone in particular. There is distortion, of course, even in our own self-images. We all deceive ourselves at times and operate out of idealized self-perceptions. But in spite of the limitations of the survey method, a well-conceived and well-executed survey gives us much to ponder.

Beyond views of peace and war, which we have already examined at length, the Brethren Member Profile probes deeper on several moral issues, among them abortion and homosexuality. Let us first consider abortion.

Abortion

When asked, "Which description *best* reflects your general outlook on the abortion issue?", nearly half (47 percent) of Brethren nationwide describe themselves as "strongly pro-life"; this is more than six times the number who say that they are "strongly pro-choice" (7.5 percent). (By comparison, about 36 percent of all Americans identify themselves as strongly pro-life, compared to nearly as many, 34 percent, who are "strongly pro-choice."[2]) These findings are presented on the left side in figure 8.2 (page 80). Consistent with their strong self-identification as pro-life, a majority of Brethren (56 percent) say that abortion is murder—as bad as killing someone who has already been born. If we add to this group persons who see abortion as less serious, but still as murder, we find that two-thirds of today's Brethren say abortion is murder. The remaining third characterize abortion as "taking human life" or "a surgical procedure," but as something less than murder. These findings are on the right in figure 8.2.

Pastors as a group are every bit as pro-life as their parishioners. Frequent Conferencegoers, however, are a different story. Those who have attended Annual Conference five or more times part company dramatically with their fellow Brethren: A majority (55 percent) view abortion as something less than murder, and nearly as many say they are pro-choice (42 percent) as pro-life (48 percent). *Messenger* subscribers, too, are notably more pro-choice than the membership in general. Most strikingly pro-choice, though, is the small group of Brethren who graduated from a Brethren college. This is one of the only Brethren contexts in which persons who call themselves "pro-choice" outnumber those who self-identify as "pro-life."

Ironically but not surprisingly, Brethren who say they are "pro-life" typically have a more positive view of military service, the armed forces, and the exercise of military force than other Brethren. Pro-life Brethren are also more supportive of the death penalty. This is noted not to make "pro-life" Brethren appear foolish or inconsistent, but to underscore the fact that both "pro-life" and "pro-choice" Brethren may draw more from conservative and progressive agendas in the culture at large than from their own Brethren faith heritage. Even the strong peace stance of some Brethren progressives may owe as much to the broader culture as to their distinctive peace heritage. It is a question worth considering.

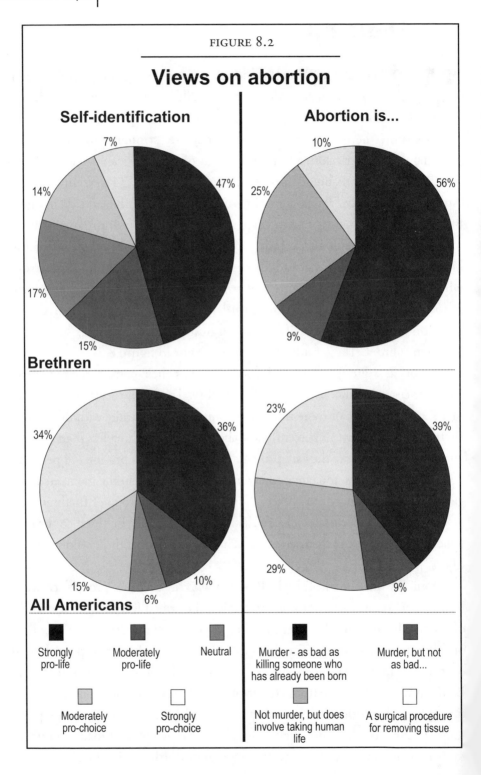

FIGURE 8.2

Views on abortion

Self-identification

7%
47%
14%
17%
15%

Brethren

Abortion is...

10%
56%
25%
9%

34%
36%
15%
10%
6%

All Americans

23%
39%
29%
9%

Strongly pro-life

Moderately pro-life

Neutral

Moderately pro-choice

Strongly pro-choice

Murder - as bad as killing someone who has already been born

Murder, but not as bad...

Not murder, but does involve taking human life

A surgical procedure for removing tissue

Human sexuality

One of the most vexing issues facing the denomination in recent years has been that of human sexuality. The fact that a landmark Annual Conference decision of nearly a quarter-century ago remains in effect is hardly a sign of calm. On the contrary, the topic has been so volatile that Brethren have had to weather grassroots movements, an Annual Conference moratorium on new business, congregational divisions, and church discipline, all sparked by a topic—homosexuality—that has Brethren like many other Americans in a state of consternation about what to do. Committed Christians on one side of the issue see homosexuality, like heterosexuality, as a gift from God. Committed Christians on the other see homosexuality as an abomination, a sin to be overcome like other sinful impulses.

Because of the polarization on this topic, it would have been easy for the Brethren Member Profile to avoid it altogether. But the judgment was made that an anonymous mail survey was one of the best methods to discern how the membership really view the topic. So Brethren were asked not only their own sexual orientation, but also to identify the congregational roles in which they would accept practicing homosexuals, and whether they agree with a number of specific statements about homosexuality. The general portrait that emerges from all of these questions is one of strong opposition with specific openings.

The incidence of self-reported homosexuality/bisexuality among Brethren is about the same as that reported in similar surveys of the nation as a whole: about 2 percent of the adult population. This does not include all Brethren who might have had homosexual experiences or fantasies; it refers only to those whose *identity* is something other than heterosexual. Laumann's benchmark survey of sexual practices in the United States reported a similar rate of self-identification, which again was fewer than the number who admitted some homosexual experience.[3] Many have critiqued Laumann's study as underestimating the incidence of homosexuality in the general population, but the criticism is based largely upon the reticence of subjects in a face-to-face interview—that is to say, limitations of the methodology—rather than upon inappropriate or inaccurate survey procedures.

While the incidence of homosexuality among Brethren may be similar to the nation as a whole, their view of homosexuality is not. Forty-four percent of Americans nationwide believe that homosexuality should be considered an acceptable alternative lifestyle, compared to 22 percent of the Brethren. In America, nearly 4 of every 10 adults (38 percent) say that homosexual couples should have the right to marry, compared to just 16 percent of the Brethren. Not only does the rate of homosexual acceptance among Brethren register at about half the rate of the general population, but the Brethren who oppose homosexuality, do so adamantly. On a spectrum ranging from "completely disagree" through "mostly disagree" and "mostly agree" to "completely agree"—60 percent of Brethren completely disagree that homosexuality should be considered an acceptable lifestyle, 63 percent completely disagree that homosexuals should be allowed to adopt children, and 71 percent completely disagree that homosexuals should have the right to marry. The comparable figures for the nation are 34 percent, 39 percent, and 43 percent, respectively. Across the nation, there is still majority opposition to a generalized acceptance of homosexuality, but it is not the unqualified opposition that stills exists among the majority of Brethren.

Brethren are less inclined than Americans as a whole to believe that individuals are hard-wired with a particular sexual orientation at birth. (Only 30 percent of Brethren hold this view, compared to 45 percent of the general population.) Few Brethren favor any type of congregational leadership for practicing homosexuals. Only 15 percent say they could accept a practicing homosexual as a lay leader, and only 11 percent—about one member in 10—say that they could accept a practicing homosexual as an ordained minister in their congregation.

It is interesting, though, that this strong opposition does not extend into certain areas that we might expect. For instance, even though three-quarters of the membership morally oppose homosexuality, half are willing to accept a practicing homosexual as a member of their local congregation.[4] (This includes 35 percent of those who say that homosexuality is *not* an acceptable lifestyle alternative.) Only a minority of Brethren (36 percent) say that homosexual behavior between consenting adults should be against the law.

Chapter 9 | Politics, patriotism, and the state

I met a Methodist once who knew little about the Brethren. She was, however, aware of their legacy as one of the three historic peace churches. She therefore assumed that Brethren would tend to affiliate with the Democratic party, to oppose military interventions of any type, and to downplay things such as patriotism and national identity. She couldn't have been more wrong.

Over half (53 percent) of today's Brethren describe their political views as "conservative," compared to only 12 percent who say they are "liberal." So self-identified conservatives outnumber liberals by more than four to one. Given this strong conservative tilt, it is not surprising that there are twice as many Republicans as Democrats in the Church of the Brethren; these party affiliations are roughly equal in the broader American population (see figure 9.1). The presidential election of 2004 was a clear victory for President George W. Bush, even though he received only 3 percent more of the popular vote than runner-up John Kerry. Had Brethren been the only voters though, Kerry could have saved his money and ended his efforts months earlier, for he received only 28 percent of the Brethren vote, compared to 48 percent nationally. President Bush was the choice of 7 of every 10 Brethren voters.[1]

Nine out of 10 Brethren say that they are at least moderately patriotic, and nearly as many (85 percent) believe that America is a force for good in the world. Brethren also overwhelmingly believe that "the world would be better off if more

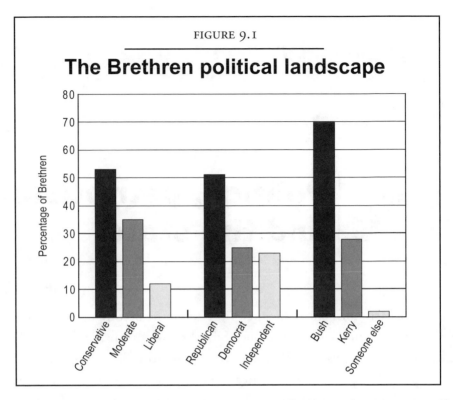

FIGURE 9.1

The Brethren political landscape

nations embraced Christianity" (90 percent); "the U.S. should remain the world's dominant military power" (74 percent); "America is a Christian nation" (73 percent); and "the United States has a special role in God's plan for the world" (72 percent). Smaller Brethren majorities support the idea that "America should help America first and the rest of the world later" (66 percent); "the U.S. armed forces should continue the fight against terror until all serious threats have been eliminated" (61 percent); "the world would be better off if more nations embraced American values" (61 percent), and "American culture is superior to most other cultures" (53 percent).

Given their view of the United States as a Christian nation and their sense of America's special role in God's divine plan, it is not surprising that few of today's Brethren have a problem with displaying the flag during worship. By more than a two-to-one margin, Brethren say that it is "all right to display the American flag inside a Brethren sanctuary." A majority of them have displayed the U.S. flag outside of their own homes.

Chapter 10 | **Whose birthday?**

Three hundred years ago in 1708, the Brethren didn't conduct scientific surveys. By 1808, few advances had been made in this regard (of course). At their bicentennial, John Gillin published a study of the Brethren that was based upon extensive reading and interaction rather than questionnaires and scientific samples. Among Gillin's observations about the church's "present condition" were:

- Their appreciation is keen in all matters that pertain to agriculture, and less keen in affairs that do not touch their immediate interests.

- In matters of education and science, they are content with theories that have been outgrown for almost a century.

- In their religion they have been nothing, if not practical. Their religion has to do with ecclesiastical policies and personal ethics, not with theology.

- The Dunker type of disposition should probably be called domineering. This type of disposition reveals itself in the reverence that is required to be paid to their older members, to the governing officials of the congregation, and to any authority whatsoever. . . .When once the church has spoken in the Annual Meeting, it becomes the duty of every member to render obedience to the decision. When a local congregation has expressed its mind on a matter, it is in bad taste, to say the least, for anyone to question the result.

- Among new and hostile surroundings, but protected by social isolation, they have clung to their beliefs, in spite of the sneers of other Christian denominations.

- They have held themselves so strictly to their ideas, and have been so earnest with their convictions that they have been intolerant of others. This has gone to such lengths that many of them believe that theirs is the only true church of Christ.

- This legalistic conception of the nature of Christianity has determined the nature of almost all the decisions of the Annual Meeting. Life is duty. The Gospel is a law of duty. How to obey this law, as well as just what this law is in its essence, has been the crux of all their troubles.

- No great poet, or philosopher, or educator was born or bred among the Dunkers during the first one hundred and fifty years of their history. But the Dunkers have produced a great mediocre class of substantial, worldly-wise, industrious, economical, peaceful, moral and religious citizens, possessed of more than the common virtues, and with few vices.

- In some congregations families intermarry generation after generation. The degree of kinship is not so close that any evil results appear in the offspring, but four or five families may intermarry for a long time without being closely related. For example, I know of three families in a congregation in which the women did not change their names, when they were married; yet they and their husbands were only very distant relatives. Occasionally, however, a Dunker marries out of the congregation. . . .

- [T]he idea that the individual exists for the church is gradually being displaced by the conception that the church exists for the welfare of the individual. The policy of coercion is gradually giving way to the policy of liberalism.[1]

If these century-old descriptions now seem strange, they are no stranger than the title of Gillin's book itself: *The Dunkers*. If these strike any remaining chords of recognition, it is primarily for the oldest among us. Only a few are historically informed enough to legitimately question some of Gillin's more questionable assertions. Others might object to the descriptions, but only because they now sound odd or unappetizing. Truth be told, they aren't the kind of historical portrait that Brethren like to celebrate.

Apart from occasional garb-strutting, pie-and-ice-cream-eating, Dunker Day celebrations, Brethren are now disengaged from their heritage by time and culture. Annual Conference, a significant sustainer and transmitter of Brethren memory, is less significant to post-baby boom Brethren, three-quarters of whom have never attended. Six out of 10 Brethren under the age of 40 say that Annual Conference decisions have little or no importance for them. So it is not surprising that the most common response when younger Brethren are asked how satisfied they are with Annual Conference is "not sure." Nearly two-thirds (63 percent) of Brethren over the age of 70 say they have a strong commitment to the Church of the Brethren nationally, compared to just 30 percent of Brethren younger than 40. This denominational detachment of younger Brethren is reflected in everything from *Messenger* subscriptions, to their attitude toward Brethren Sunday school material, to their level of concern about whether their local congregation remains Brethren. On many different indicators, Brethren younger than 40 have about half the denominational attachment of Brethren over 70. In 1986, I wrote about "the declining importance of being Brethren." In 2007, this pattern sharply persists.

For denominations born of a less radical, less sectarian impulse, this is still problematic, but less so than it is for the Brethren. Brethren have always defined themselves to a large degree in terms of their dissent from mainstream Christianity. One hundred years ago, at their bicenntennial, everything from their worship, to their buildings, to their political participation, to their very clothing was cut from a distinctive cloth. It was a cloth, as many have repeated in recent years, "kind of like the Mennonites," but with a less hierarchical leadership structure, stronger efforts to preserve national unity, and more emphasis upon certain outward ordinances. Brethren knew that, like the Mennonites, they were a peace people and a simple people. They were suspicious of anything that could be interpreted as "easy" Christianity, which is one reason they were just beginning to cooperate with groups like the Methodists, Presbyterians, and Baptists. They had not yet fully embraced voting in civil elections or paying ministers a salary. Annual Meeting still characterized the church of Jesus Christ as "no part of this world system." Brethren were called to be "in the world but of the church," to consider their "citizenship being in heaven," and to sustain "the attitude of a pilgrim" to the affairs of state.[2]

At the 250th anniversary celebration, 50 years ago, Brethren were strongly challenged by Kermit Eby to preserve their distinctiveness. In *The Adventurous Future*, a collection of essays compiled for the celebration, Eby wrote, "Our ancestor's greatness lay in their uniqueness—in belief, character, and witness. The uniqueness of a Dunker, at its best, involved more than his mode of dress. As much, it included the 'queerness' of the man who lived in the world by otherworldly standards." By 1958, the Christian "queerness" to which Eby refers had largely vanished, as he acknowledged later in the same essay—"Conformity to the world's values, and not tension or conflict with them, is true of us today; we have come full cycle." Even though this greatly concerned him, remaining areas of Brethren distinction, like pacifism, gave Eby cause for hope. His challenge to the Brethren was razor sharp, for he warned them that "Brethren, if they *cannot* be unique, *can* be nothing."[3]

In 1986, Annual Conference moderator Donald F. Durnbaugh challenged Brethren to strengthen their witness by suggesting that the only thing they still had in common was the fact that they all owned televisions.[4] Like Eby and a long list of 20th-century Brethren leaders—from eastern Pennsylvania elders such as J. H. Longenecker and S. H. Hertzler to Dan West, Anna Mow, M. R. Zigler, Vernard Eller, Dale Brown, and others—Durnbaugh hoped for a prophetic witness to the future that would be grounded in a historical consciousness of the Brethren's heritage of dissent. His words and tactics were subtler than Kermit Eby's, but their purposes shared much in common. Both took issue with historical shifts that trended toward "Brethren Lite," for want of a better term.

As we have seen in this report of the 2006 Brethren Member Profile, Church of the Brethren members are still widely scattered in their understandings of the essence of the faith. Some continue to treasure elements of a distinctive Anabaptist-Pietist heritage, while many others do not. Some celebrate the breadth of this diversity, while others interpret it as the loss of what made Brethren *Brethren*. Among the latter are those who place special emphasis upon the second part of Christ's great commission: "teaching them to obey everything that I have commanded you" (Matt. 28:20). Such Brethren raise the question "Beyond faith in Christ, what shall we teach? What are the practical implications of that faith? How will they know we are Brethren?" If Gillin was correct one hundred years ago when he observed that the Brethren had a particularly practical faith, this would be a harder argument to make today. To the extent that the faith is still practical, it elicits widely different practices from different Brethren.

This much is certain. The Brethren identity in itself is deeply valued, even if the substance of that identity varies from congregation to congregation, location to location. "Brethren" is by far the favorite description, when members are asked to select words or labels to describe their faith. And when members are asked explicitly about the name—Would you favor or oppose changing the name of the Church of the Brethren to a new name that does not include the word "Brethren"?—fewer than one member in 20 (4 percent) favor changing the name. Seventy-five percent, on the other hand, oppose such a change, while the remaining 21 percent are unsure. Were Donald Durnbaugh alive today, he might point out that Brethren are clear that they want to remain Brethren; they simply can't decide what it means.

Afterword

Carl Bowman has offered us a brief, yet challenging, interpretation of the Brethren Member Profile 2006. The results show that, in most ways, the trends he noted in the 1980s have continued. Overall these trends point to a continued relativizing and diminishing of distinctiveness in faith and practice in the Church of the Brethren, even though its members still identify themselves with the label "Brethren."

As Bowman indicates, this book is a beginning. While the questionnaire was carefully constructed and distributed and the return rate is sufficient to give a solid base of data, interpretation will continue. Readers can look forward to more interpretive work on the survey results from Bowman and others.

Meanwhile, now is a time for all Brethren to engage in interpreting the significance of the data. The book offers many openings for Brethren to talk about what they believe and what difference their faith makes in their actions. Some may celebrate Bowman's findings, namely that the trends of the last 20 years have stayed the same. According to the survey, many Brethren now think that denominations are unimportant, even if they might choose the name "Brethren" as the best description for themselves. For much of the 20th century, especially after World War II, some Brethren have tried valiantly to erase or dilute what has been distinctive about our church. These results might come as welcome confirmation to those who favor such efforts.

Bowman has not offered us celebration, however. Indeed, Brethren who have seen our church as offering something distinctive in the family of Christianity will hear clearly the warnings that Bowman has cited from the voices of leaders such as Kermit Eby, Donald Durnbaugh, and Dale Brown. For such Brethren, the results only intensify the concerns over losses of distinctiveness in faith.

Whether one sees the survey results as a glass half empty or a glass half full, or some of both, this book challenges Brethren to talk and pray about what they wish the future to be like in light of God's leading, and to act. In presenting Brethren with the fairly honest picture that they provide of themselves, Bowman's book challenges us both to consider whether this is the kind of church that Brethren want and to remember that none of these trends is inevitable. As Bowman's book *Brethren Society* (based in part on the previous profile of Brethren members) described so well, the changes of the 20th century took decades to complete. Few of those changes happened uncontested. All of them came about from a mix of intentional planning and leadership, compromise, apathy—and sometimes by accident.

As we celebrate the Brethren tricentennial, we are no less bound to inevitability than the church was a hundred years ago. What is clearer in this current book is that Brethren don't agree on what trends they find desirable to retain, and which ones they might like to change. In a few cases, readers might wonder if church members know enough about the patterns of the present to discern what they desire. This book puts into the hands of Brethren (and others) a useful package of well-supported data to inform us about these patterns. As Brethren begin a new century, the time is urgent to discern what is faithful for the future.

Jeffrey A. Bach
The Young Center for Anabaptist and Pietist Studies
Elizabethtown College

Notes

Chapter 1: Introduction

1. "American Piety in the 21st Century: Selected Findings from the Baylor Religion Survey" from *The Baylor Institute for Studies of Religion*, September 2006, p. 9.

2. This study is part of the larger *Church Member Profile 2006*, based at Elizabethtown College's Young Center for Anabaptist and Pietist Studies, of which Donald B. Kraybill is the senior project director. The other denominations participating in the broader study are the Mennonite Church USA and the Brethren in Christ.

Chapter 2: Where are the Brethren?

1. According to national membership statistics for 2005, median congregation size is 88 members. The median for congregations of average worship attendance is 60.

2. Based upon 2005 average attendance figures, 17 percent attend congregations that have 50 or fewer worshiping on an average Sunday, and 22 percent attend congregations that have an average attendance of 200 or more. Only 13 percent attend congregations with an average attendance of more than 250.

Chapter 3: Theology

1. Only 9 percent take the position that "God does not bless nations."

R. Eberly, ed., *The Complete Writings of Alexander Mack* (Wi-
Lake, Ind.: BMH Books, 1991), 25.

or additional reference, see the 1998 Annual Conference statement en-
titled "The New Testament as Our Rule of Faith and Practice," available
online at http://www.brethren.org/ac/ac_statements/98NewTestament
.htm.

Chapter 4: Brethren connections

1. The following table shows the distribution of Brethren roots. These are
hierarchical categories, meaning that those in category 2 did not meet the
condition in category 1, those in category 3 did not meet the condition
in category 2, etc. So category 5, for example, contains respondents who
had no Brethren ancestry of their own, but who married someone who
was raised Brethren.

Brethren ancestry variable	Frequency	Percent	Cumulative percentage
1. All grandparents Brethren on both sides	197.48	10.83	100.00
2. Have Brethren grandparents on both sides	188.68	10.34	89.17
3. Have at least one Brethren parent *and* grandparent	559.13	30.65	78.83
4. Have at least one Brethren ancestor	231.53	12.69	48.18
5. Married someone who was raised Brethren	257.87	14.14	35.49
6. No Brethren family connection	389.52	21.35	21.35

2. Only 16 percent of those younger than 50 have attended more than
once.

3. All of these percentages are the percentage of those who attended a Brethren college who selected each school. The number of persons in the sample under age 50 who attended a Brethren college is small enough tha
these percentages should not be generalized beyond the sample.

4. "Frequent attenders" are those who have attended Annual Conference
more than two times, while "non-attenders" have never attended.

Chapter 6: Church ordinances and worship

1. Eberly, *The Complete Writings of Alexander Mack*, 13.

2. Twenty-eight percent of Brethren under age 35 say that feetwashing

awkward and uncomfortable, compared to 11 percent of Brethren 65 and older. Only half of Brethren under age 35 say that feetwashing is spiritually moving and very meaningful, compared to 70 percent of Brethren 65 and over. In contrast, 43 percent of Brethren under age 35 say that feetwashing builds a deep sense of church community, compared to 29 percent of Brethren 65 and older.

3. Eberly, *The Complete Writings of Alexander Mack*, 19. To add clarity, the word "Brethren" has been substituted for "Baptist" because Mack was writing about his brethren.

4. Sixty percent of Brethren reject the idea of infant baptism on survey question E18b *and also* say that adult baptism is either fairly or very important to them on question B25d. If we add to this the 9 percent of Brethren who are neutral on E18b, but say that adult baptism is very important to them on B25d, the percent of Brethren committed to adult baptism is 69 percent, or 7 out of 10.

5. Based upon reported worship attendance of respondents to the Brethren Member Profile study, one would estimate that on an average Sunday, just over 100,000 members nationwide attend worship at a Brethren congregation. The comparable figure reported by the denomination for 2005 is just over 65,000. The denomination, however, has worship attendance estimates for only three-quarters of its congregations. If we adjust the denomination's 65,000 figure upward to compensate for incomplete data, the estimated number in attendance would be around 80,000. Even with this adjustment, we find the Brethren Member Profile estimate to be overly optimistic, suggesting that the sample is somewhat skewed toward those who are more actively involved in their congregations, and that their answers to the questionnaire tend to cast a "best light" upon their activities and involvements.

Another indication of this is that the number of *Messenger* subscriptions nationwide in October 2006, subtracting those that go to libraries and organizations, is approximately 12,000. By comparison, 30 percent of our sample reported receiving *Messenger* at home. If 30 percent of the national membership of approximately 129,000 actually received the magazine at home, the subscription rate would be three times higher than the actual figure of 12,000. That stated, the 129,000 membership figure reported by the denomination is only a "best estimate" based upon incomplete data and figures that are extrapolated from previous years with adjustments for baptisms and withdrawals.

Given these comparisons with national data, the best way to think of the Brethren Member Profile sample is to consider it a representative sample of more actively involved Brethren members. In fact, the Brethren Member Profile worship attendance estimates suggest that a national membership figure of about 100,000 relatively active members might be a better estimate of the genuine, or vital, membership than the number reported by the General Board, based on information submitted by congregations.

6. The 1985 Brethren Profile Study reported that 72 percent of the membership attended worship on a weekly basis, a number virtually identical to the 71 percent reported by this study.

Chapter 7: Peace and military service

1. Slightly abridged excerpt from the Annual Meeting Minutes, 1785, Article 1.
2. Constructed from "The Testament of William Knepper," written during the early 1740s. Carl F. Bowman, *Brethren Society: The Cultural Transformation of a "Peculiar People"* (Baltimore, Md.: The Johns Hopkins University Press, 1995), 24-25.
3. "A Restatement Concerning War and Peace," Annual Conference Minutes, 1935.
4. "Position and Practices of the Church of the Brethren in Relation to War," Annual Conference Minutes, 1948.
5. "Statement of the Church of the Brethren on War," Annual Conference Minutes, 1970.
6. "Peacemaking: The Calling of God's People in History," Annual Conference Minutes, 1991.
7. Jesse H. Ziegler, *The Broken Cup: Three Generations of Dunkers* (Elgin, Ill.: Brethren Publishing House, 1942), 119.
8. The recommendation to counsel Brethren is contained in the Annual Conference Minutes, 1991, "Peacemaking: The Calling of God's People in History" (284-311). The likely position of Brethren a decade or two

earlier than the 1980s is based upon the fact that, according to the Brethren Member Study, 35 percent of Brethren who were 65 and older held such a view during the 1980s.

9. During March 2006, 45 percent of Americans nationally said that the U.S. "made the right decision in using military force against Iraq." *Pew Research Center for the People & the Press, June 2006 News Interest/ Believability Final Topline.* http://people-press.org/reports/questionnaires/278.pdf.

10. The percentages for these are 92 percent, 86 percent, and 91 percent of members, respectively.

11. The percentage of respondents who favor one of the three non-military options is 37 percent if those who neglected to respond to the question are excluded from the percentage calculation, which is the general practice for percentages reported in this study. However, if those who didn't respond are included in the percentage calculation, only 33.9 percent chose a nonmilitary option. A general analysis of respondents who left items blank suggests that they are generally disinterested and less invested in Brethren heritage and doctrine. This, combined with any nonresponse bias introduced by the fact that one-third of those surveyed failed to return the questionnaire, suggests that one-third of the national membership may be a realistic estimate of the proportion of *active* members who would favor a nonmilitary option, but is probably an overestimate for the total national membership (including active and inactive members).

12. Eberly, *The Complete Writings of Alexander Mack*, 38.

13. Ibid., 82.

14. Ibid., 86.

15. Rufus D. Bowman, *Seventy Times Seven* (Elgin, Ill.: Brethren Publishing House, 1945), 131.

16. Floyd E. Mallott, *Studies in Brethren History* (Elgin, Ill.: Brethren Publishing House, 1954), 273-74.

17. Dale W. Brown, *Another Way of Believing: A Brethren Theology* (Elgin, Ill.: Brethren Press, 2005), 232.

18. Jimmy Carter, *Our Endangered Values: America's Moral Crisis* (New York: Simon and Schuster, 2005), 147.

Chapter 8: The "moral issues"

1. For the purposes of this discussion, "elderly" denotes Brethren older than 70, and "young" denotes Brethren younger than 40.

2. These figures are from a representative national omnibus poll conducted in December 2005 by RT Strategies of Arlington, Virginia. March 7, 2007. http://www.cookpolitical.com/races/report_pdfs/2005_poll_tl_dec12.pdf.

3. Laumann, Edward O., et al., *The Social Organization of Sexuality: Sexual Practices in the United States* (Chicago: University of Chicago Press, 1994).

4. Respondents who failed to question C27a and to question C27d were eliminated from the basis for this reported percentage, the reasoning being that they were skipping the questioning, rather than responding that they were unwilling to accept homosexuals as members.

Chapter 9: Politics, patriotism, and the state

1. In the Brethren Political Landscape chart, the "Independent" bar includes Brethren who self-identified as Independent *and* those who said they have no party affiliation. Percentages for Bush and Kerry are based upon Brethren who voted in the election, rather than all Brethren.

Chapter 10: Whose birthday?

1. John Lewis Gillin, *The Dunkers: A Sociological Interpretation* (New York, 1906). These direct quotes from Gillin are excerpted from the chapter on "present conditions," pages 203 to 224.

2. "Statement on Voting and Politics," Annual Meeting Minutes, 1912.

3. Kermit Eby, "The Brethren and Their Culture," in *The Adventurous Future: A compilation of addresses, papers, statements, and messages associated with the celebration of the two-hundred-fiftieth anniversary of the Church of the Brethren*, ed. Paul H. Bowman (Elgin, Ill.: The Brethren Press, 1959), 145, 147, and 152 respectively.

4. Durnbaugh based this conclusion in the findings of the 1985 Brethren Profile Study, a nationally representative survey of the Brethren membership.

Research
methodology

The sample of members was drawn in two stages. First a representative sample of congregations was selected, with the probability of selection being determined by the congregation's size, and then a random sample of members was selected from within the sampled congregations.

Before the sampling of congregations was undertaken, all Church of the Brethren congregations in the continental United States were sorted into "bins," so to speak, based upon their geographic location (district) and the size of the congregation. This technique, referred to in sampling as "stratification," was employed to ensure that all sizes and geographic locations would be included in the final sample. Then a congregation was selected from each bin using a computer-assisted technique whereby the probability of selection varied according to the size of the congregation. One-hundred and thirty congregations were selected in this fashion, 106 of which agreed to participate in the study. Since this left 24 congregational bins without a representative, replacement congregations were selected using the same procedure. In the end, 127 of our 130 congregational bins were represented by a congregation that agreed to participate.

These congregations were asked to supply membership lists, from which a total of 2,961 Church of the Brethren members were selected. Typically, about 30 members were randomly selected from each congregation in the sample, with the exception being very small congregations, from which the number was smaller. The names, addresses, and phone numbers of these individuals were input into a database at the Young Center, and the resulting list was checked for inaccuracies against lists supplied by the United States Postal Service.

The questionnaire, which contained 17 full pages requesting approximately 500 different pieces of information, was mailed on February 16, 2006. A follow-up thank-you/reminder postcard was mailed to all recipients on February 24. As each questionnaire was received, it was pulled from its return envelope, preventing any possibility of identifying who had responded to the questionnaire. The empty return envelopes, which had a code number, were then used to record who had responded and to compile a list of non-respondents. On March 9, a second reminder postcard was sent to the 1,898 Brethren who had not yet responded. About two and a half weeks later, on March 27, a second complete copy of the questionnaire was mailed to the 1,263 members who still had not responded. If it sounds like we were relentless in pursuing responses, we were.

On May 15, three months after the mailing of the first questionnaire, the data collection phase was closed. No questionnaires were accepted after that date. At final tally, 1,826 Brethren had completed and returned their questionnaires, which was 66 percent of the 2,758 potential respondents (after the initial sample of 2,961 had been adjusted to account for congregations that did not participate, and individuals who were no longer members).

Weights were devised to account for different rates of response between congregations. What this means is that if congregation X had a return rate of 15 out of 30, while congregation Y had a return rate of 25 out of 30, the responses from congregation X were given additional weight (in direct proportion to the amount that they had "under-responded") in the tallying of final responses. Such an adjustment ensures the correct balance of geographic and congregational representation that the sampling procedure was designed to accomplish. A similar adjustment was employed to compensate for differential response rates between genders.

Unfortunately, the design of this survey offers little opportunity to analyze the mix of ethnic minorities in the Church of the Brethren. The questionnaire itself is in English, which precluded a direct mail survey of Latino or Haitian members. Consultation with African American pastors also suggested that the direct-mail format would prove ineffective in those congregations, which it did. There were insufficient funds to conduct a separate survey of Latinos, Haitians, Dominicans, and African Americans using something other than the impersonal, direct-mail approach. Such an effort would be valuable and remains to be accomplished. This noted, it is also unfortunate that these ethnic minorities constitute such a small proportion of the total Church of the Brethren membership. *Esperamos que el futuro nos presente otra realidad en ese respeto.*

The data were analyzed using SYSTAT software.

Brethren Membership Profile

A Study of Beliefs and Practices

These pages report the pattern of response to each question in the Brethren Membership Profile. The number in **bold** beside an answer is the percentage of the Brethren members who gave that response. We have preserved the question ordering and wording from the mailed questionnaire. Formatting, however, had to be adapted to the smaller page size of this book.

Full survey results

CMP2006
CHURCH MEMBER PROFILE

A Study of Beliefs and Practices

SECTION A: FAITH CONNECTIONS

Check **ONE** answer box for each question, unless other directions are provided.

1. **How important to you are your religious beliefs?**

   0 Not at all important
   1 Not too important
   8 Fairly important
   56 Very important
   35 The most important thing in my life

2. **About how many years altogether have you been a baptized member of the Church of the Brethren?**
   (write) about _____ years

   20 10 years or less
   30 11-30 years
   50 More than 30

3. **Were you ever a member of a non-Brethren congregation?**

   60 No
   40 Yes

   IF YES, in which denomination or independent church were you most recently a member?
   (write) _____

   _____

4. **About how old were you when you were first baptized?**
   (write) _____ years of age

   19 <10 years
   60 10-17 years
   21 18 or older

5. **In what church were you baptized?**

   69 A Church of the Brethren congregation
   31 Some other church
   (write name of church)

   _____

6. **How often did you attend church services when you were about 12 years old?**

   3 Never
   1 Once a year or less
   7 A few times a year
   3 About once a month
   13 2 or 3 times a month
   61 Every week
   11 Several times a week

7. **Were your <u>parents</u> members of the Church of the Brethren when you were growing up?**

   43 Neither was a member.
   3 Father was, mother was not.
   10 Mother was, father was not.
   43 Both parents were members.
   2 Not sure

8. **Were your <u>mother's</u> parents members of a Brethren congregation when she was growing up?**

   56 Neither was a member.
   6 One of them was a member.
   27 Both were members.
   12 Not sure

9. **Were your <u>father's</u> parents members of a Brethren congregation when he was growing up?**

   56 Neither was a member.
   5 One of them was a member.
   26 Both were members.
   14 Not sure

10. **Think for a moment about your five closest friends outside your family. To the best of your knowledge...**

a. How many of the five participate in some faith community? *(circle number)*

   3 0
   4 1
   10 2
   16 3
   20 4
   47 5

b. How many of the five are members of the Church of the Brethren? *(circle number)*

   28 0
   18 1
   16 2
   18 3
   11 4
   10 5

c. How many of the five attend your local congregation? *(circle number)*

   35 0
   18 1
   16 2
   14 3
   9 4
   8 5

11. **Which statement <u>best</u> describes your current relationship with your Brethren congregation?** *(check one)*

   77 I am an active member.
   18 I am an inactive member.
   2 I attend, but I am not a member.
   2 I am not affiliated with a Brethren congregation.

SECTION B: RELIGIOUS BELIEFS

1. Which statement <u>best</u> expresses your belief about God? *(check one)*

- 87 I know that God really exists and I have no doubts about it.
- 11 While I have doubts, I feel that I do believe in God.
- 2 I don't believe in a personal God, but I do believe in a higher power of some kind.
- 1 I don't know whether there is a God, and I don't believe there is any way to find out.
- 0 I don't believe in God.

2. In general, how close would you describe your present relationship with God?

- 1 Very distant
- 2 Fairly distant
- 12 Neither distant nor close
- 41 Fairly close
- 44 Very close

3. Which statement <u>best</u> expresses how you think God relates to the world today? *(check one)*

- 49 God controls most of the events in my daily life.
- 39 God guides me, but does not control the events of my daily life.
- 1 God intervenes in the big events of the world, but not in my daily life.
- 4 God sees things in the world but does not intervene in them.
- 8 Not sure

4. When you pray, do you pray more often to Jesus, more often to God, or equally to both?

- 8 More often to Jesus
- 44 More often to God
- 46 About equally to both
- 2 Do not really pray to either

5. Which statements reflect your views of Jesus? *(check <u>all that apply</u>)*

- 60 I seek to be a disciple of Jesus in my daily living.
- 48 I have a close, personal relationship with Christ.
- 82 I think of Jesus as my personal Lord and Savior.
- 9 I think of Jesus as a radical social activist.
- 39 I eagerly anticipate Jesus' return to earth.
- 43 I think of Jesus as a nonviolent peacemaker.
- 34 I have an intimate spiritual connection with Jesus.
- 12 I think of Jesus in a fairly general way.
- 1 I really do not think much about Jesus.

6. Was there ever a time in your life when you accepted Christ as Savior and Lord?

- 4 No, I don't think of myself as having "accepted Christ."
- 40 Yes, it was a specific moment.
- 57 Yes, but it happened gradually over time.

7. **Which statement <u>best</u> expresses your view of the uniqueness of Jesus?** *(check one)*

   64 Jesus is the only way to God and those without faith in Jesus will not be saved.

   22 Jesus is the clearest revelation of God, but God may save people who don't know Jesus.

   11 Jesus is one of many ways to God.

   2 Jesus was a great teacher and prophet, but not more than that.

8. **Which statement best expresses your view of Jesus' divinity?** *(check one)*

   73 Jesus is fully divine and fully God.

   22 Jesus is divine, but he is not exactly God.

   4 Jesus is not divine, but he helped to reveal God to us.

   1 I don't think of Jesus as being divine.

9. **In your view, which Testament in the Bible has the highest authority?**

   5 The Old Testament
   49 The New Testament
   46 Both have equal authority.

10. **What is your most favorite passage of scripture?**
    (write) _____
    _____

11. Please indicate if you believe or do not believe each statement below.
(check one box for each statement)

	Do Believe	Do Not Believe	Not Sure
a. Jesus was born of a virgin.	90	3	6
b. Jesus physically arose from the dead.	92	98	5
c. Jesus will physically return to earth some day.	83	4	13
d. Jesus will ultimately triumph over evil.	92	2	6
e. The miracles in the Bible are historical facts.	77	7	16
f. God performs the same kind of miracles today as in the Bible.	73	7	20
g. Human nature is basically sinful.	71	17	11
h. People have a soul.	98	1	2
i. Evil is an active force in the world today.	95	2	3
j. The devil, as a personal being, is active in the world today.	81	8	10
k. Angels are active in the world today.	84	3	13
l. The Holy Spirit is active in the world today.	95	1	4
m. The Antichrist is active in the world today.	57	12	32
n. There is life after death.	90	2	8
o. Humans will see their dead loved ones in the afterlife.	73	4	23
p. Humans are reincarnated and live again on earth.	6	72	22
q. There is a real heaven where some people are eternally rewarded.	86	4	10
r. There is a real hell where some people are eternally punished.	75	9	16
s. At the rapture, saved persons will join Jesus, while others will be left behind.	75	9	16
t. God's love will one day restore all souls, even non-believers, to God.	27	43	30

12. Which statement best expresses what you believe about the Bible?

45 The Bible is the <u>actual</u> Word of God and is to be taken <u>literally</u>, word for word.

46 The Bible is the <u>inspired</u> Word of God, but not everything in it should be taken literally.

9 The Bible is an ancient book of stories, history, and moral guidelines recorded by human authors.

0 The Bible has no relevance for today.

13. In your view, does salvation depend more on what a person believes or on how a person lives? *(check one)*

27 Salvation depends more on what a person believes.

12 Salvation depends more on how a person lives.

60 Salvation depends equally on one's beliefs and how one lives.

14. If someone were to ask, "Are you saved?," which statement best reflects how you would probably respond? *(check one)*

6 "Being saved" is not central to my faith.

27 I can't say for sure; only God knows if I am saved.

3 The people who know me best can answer that better than I.

65 Yes, I know I am saved.

15. Which statement best describes your view of how human life began? *(check one)*

69 God created human beings in their present form at creation.

21 God created life and guided the emergence of humans over millions of years.

4 Humans naturally evolved from other forms of life over millions of years.

7 Not sure

16. Which statement best describes your view of how the Holy Spirit works? *(check one)*

39 The Spirit speaks directly to individuals in a personal way.

51 The Spirit speaks to individuals directly, and also through the faith community.

3 The Spirit speaks primarily through the faith community.

8 The Spirit is another name for human insight or inspiration.

17. Which statement best expresses your view of the charismatic gifts of the Holy Spirit, such as healing, prophesying, and speaking in tongues? *(check one)*

11 They are only expressions of human emotions.

16 They reflect human emotions more than God's Spirit.

9 They reflect God's Spirit more than human emotions.

64 They are genuine gifts of God's Spirit to some Christians.

18. Which of these gifts of the Spirit have you ever personally received? *(check all that apply)*

43 The "baptism of the Spirit"

4 The ability to speak in tongues

4 The gift of prophesy

2 The power to cast out demons

3 The power to heal others

47 None of the above

19. IF YOU HAVE EVER SPOKEN IN TONGUES, when was the last time? *(check one)*

2 Within the last month

0 Within the last year

1 Within the last 2 to 5 years

1 More than 5 years ago

20. Which of the following words describe your religious faith?
(check all that apply)

Note: For each word, the number before the slash is the percentage for question 20, and the number after, for question 21.

10 / 6 Fundamentalist
19 / 10 Anabaptist
15 / 11 Evangelical
83 / 64 Brethren
4 / 2 Charismatic
10 / 8 Inclusive
7 / 2 Dunker
40 / 45 Spiritual
2 / 1 Radical
1 / 1 Agnostic
4 / 1 Pietist
2 / 1 Pentecostal
14 / 8 Mainline Protestant
18 / 16 Plain living
9 / 8 Other *(write)* _____

21. Please write the two words from the list above that best describe your religious faith.

1. _____
2. _____

22. Which word <u>best</u> describes your overall religious beliefs and orientation?

45 Conservative
44 Moderate
11 Liberal

23. Would you describe yourself as a "born-again" Christian?

23 No
59 Yes
18 Not sure

24. Which statement <u>best</u> reflects how you think Christians should relate to popular culture? *(check one)*

19 Avoid it as much as possible
33 Participate in it, but not let it shape them
45 Engage it and try to make it better
4 Celebrate and affirm it

25. How important is each of the following to you in your personal faith commitments? *(check one box for each statement)*

	Not at All Important	Not Very Important	Fairly Important	Very Important
a. Following Jesus in daily life	1	3	19	78
b. Praising and glorifying God	1	5	22	72
c. Living a simple lifestyle	2	11	47	41
d. Adult (rather than infant) baptism	4	9	28	60
e. Evangelizing non-believers	4	16	37	43
f. Peacemaking and nonviolence	1	7	36	56
g. Building strong bonds of community in the church	1	4	32	63
h. Avoiding sin	1	2	18	79
i. Serving others within the church	1	3	33	63
j. Serving others outside the church	1	3	36	60
k. Giving and receiving counsel from other members	2	13	49	36
l. Nonconformity to the world	3	18	40	40
m. Promoting social justice in the world	2	12	48	39
n. Expressing Christian love in all my relationships	1	3	23	73
o. Spiritual growth	1	3	20	77
p. Practicing the spiritual disciplines	1	6	30	63

26. How much do you agree or disagree with these statements?
(check one box for each statement)

	Completely Disagree	Mostly Disagree	Mostly Agree	Completely Agree
a. Too much emphasis on Brethren beliefs gets in the way of the true message of the Gospel.	18	38	35	9
b. All views of what is good are equally valid.	19	24	45	12
c. Christians should do all they can to convert non-believers to Christ.	5	12	38	45
d. Muslims and Christians worship the same God.	39	22	100	14
e. Church denominations do not matter to me; one is as good as another.	19	31	40	10
f. The organized church does not really matter; personal faith is what counts.	13	30	36	20
g. The greatest moral virtue is to be honest about your own feelings and desires.	10	19	40	30
h. God has a specific plan for my life.	2	5	29	64
i. God blesses faithful Christians with financial rewards.	29	35	26	9
j. Spiritual warfare between the forces of Satan and God is real in my life.	10	16	36	38
k. Church leaders should try to influence government leaders on issues like war, peace, racism, and poverty.	6	14	49	30
l. Church of the Brethren teachings more accurately reflect God's Word than the teachings of other denominations.	11	34	44	8
m. All war is sin.	15	28	34	22
n. There is a clear difference between the "kingdom of God" and the "kingdoms of this world."	1	4	28	65
o. Christians should avoid involvements in the "kingdoms of this world" as much as possible.	6	28	40	25
p. Old Order groups such as the Amish provide an important Christian witness in modern society.	5	23	51	20

SECTION C: RELIGIOUS ACTIVITIES AND CONGREGATIONAL LIFE

1. How often do you typically attend worship services?

- **1** Never
- **2** Once a year or less
- **8** A few times a year
- **3** About once a month
- **15** 2 or 3 times a month
- **60** Every week
- **11** Several times a week

2. How often do you typically attend Sunday School?

- **29** Never
- **6** Once a year or less
- **11** A few times a year
- **3** About once a month
- **9** 2 or 3 times a month
- **42** Every week

3. How positive or negative do you feel about having these items as a regular part of your worship service? *(check one box for each item)*

	Very Negative	Negative	Neutral	Positive	Very Positive
a. Hymns with 4-part harmony	1	4	38	31	26
b. Contemporary praise songs	2	8	34	35	21
c. Personal faith testimonies	1	8	33	39	19
d. Kneeling for prayer	3	14	51	22	10
e. Raising hands in praise	4	17	48	21	10
f. Singing without instruments (a cappella)	3	11	47	29	11
g. Altar calls with people going forward	2	7	28	35	27
h. Organ music	1	2	22	44	31
i. Electric guitars and drums	5	13	40	29	13
j. Projecting images or lyrics on a large screen	5	14	39	27	15
k. Drama and dance	10	21	39	22	7
l. Applauding singers or musicians	4	12	30	37	17
m. Litanies and responsive readings	2	5	31	48	15
n. Other people praying aloud while the minister prays	16	44	32	7	2
o. Referring to God as "Mother" or "She"	49	28	18	4	2
p. Referring to God as "Father" or "He"	3	3	20	32	42

4. **How often do you do each of the following activities?** *(check one box for each activity)*

	Never	Several Times a Year	Once a Month	2-3 Times a Month	Once a Week	Several Times a Week	Daily
a. Read or study the Bible on your own	9	20	5	9	13	22	22
b. Pray privately	1	3	2	4	4	20	66
c. Have devotions with family members	45	21	5	6	6	9	8
d. Say grace (pray) before meals	6	16	3	6	5	16	48
e. Participate in a small group for discussion, prayer, or Bible study (other than family or Sunday School)	40	23	7	8	17	3	2
f. Attend services at a non-Brethren congregation	35	55	3	3	4	1	1
g. Speak about your faith to persons outside your church and family	11	39	12	16	7	11	4
h. Try to convert others to faith in Christ	41	36	5	8	3	5	3
i. Invite others to attend services or activities at your church	17	53	9	11	4	4	3
j. Seek the Holy Spirit's guidance	6	12	3	6	5	17	50
k. Show others what it means to follow Jesus	14	18	4	7	4	12	40

5. **All things considered, would you prefer to use Sunday School materials published by the Brethren or by another Christian publisher?**

   32 Prefer Brethren materials
   10 Prefer materials by another Christian publisher
   58 No preference for who publishes the materials

6. **In a typical week, about how many hours do you spend in activities related to your congregation, beyond worship services?** *(write)* about _____ hours

   Median: just over <u>1</u> hour

7. **Many Brethren congregations celebrate both a "bread and cup" communion during worship and a separate Love Feast that includes feetwashing and a meal. Which do you prefer?**

29 I prefer bread and cup communion.

37 I prefer the Love Feast.

34 I have no preference.

8. **Over the past five years, how often have you attended the traditional Brethren Love Feast (which includes feetwashing, a meal, and communion)?**

39 More than once a year

26 About once a year

12 Less than once a year

23 Not in the last five years

9. **Which statements express your personal view of feetwashing?** *(check all that apply)*

17 It is awkward and uncomfortable.

7 It is an outdated service that should fade away.

65 It is spiritually moving and very meaningful.

33 It builds a deep sense of church community.

10. **Which statement best express-es your view of who should be allowed to participate in the communion service during Love Feast?** *(check only one)*

2 Only the members of my congregation

4 Only members of the Church of the Brethren

12 Anyone who holds membership in a Christian church

55 Anyone who accepts Jesus as Savior and Lord

1 Believers of any faith, such as Jews, Muslims, and Hindus

26 Anyone who wishes to participate

11. **Do you think that young children should be permitted to participate in the full Love Feast?**

30 Yes

35 No

35 Not sure

12. **Which, if any, of these positions have you ever held in any Church of the Brethren congregation?** *(check all that apply)*

27 Worship or music leader

54 Sunday school teacher

23 Youth adviser

25 Deacon

4 Pastor

1 Elder

4 Licensed or ordained minister

49 Church board member

39 Member of a church choir or handbell group

22 Director of a program (e.g., worship, education, missions, youth)

26 Delegate to District Conference

13. **When you think about leader-ship in your own congregation, which pattern do you prefer?**
(check one)

   35 One salaried pastor <u>with</u> additional salaried staff
   30 One salaried pastor <u>without</u> additional salaried staff
   14 A salaried team of ministers and staff
   1 One non-salaried minister
   3 A non-salaried team of ministers
   17 Not sure

14. **Would you prefer to have a pastor selected from within your congregation or from outside it?**

   18 Selected from within
   27 Selected from outside
   55 No preference

15. **Which type of ministry education do you prefer for a pastor?**
(check one)

   3 Entirely self-educated through personal Bible study and prayer
   7 Formal Bible and ministry classes, but not at the seminary level
   20 Formal Bible classes and some seminary training beyond college
   40 Completion of a seminary degree
   30 No preference

16. **IF YOU PREFER A SEMINARY EDUCATED PASTOR, would you prefer a pastor educated at Bethany Theological Seminary (the Church of the Brethren seminary) or at some other seminary?**

   29 I prefer that my pastor's education be from Bethany.
   5 I prefer that my pastor's education be from some other seminary.
   66 I have no preference.

17. **How important is it to you that your pastor emphasize distinctive Brethren beliefs and practices?**

   7 Not at all important
   19 Not very important
   43 Fairly important
   32 Very important

18. **Which statement best reflects your view of women in pastoral roles?**

   11 Women should never fill any pastoral roles.
   19 Women may fill some pastoral roles, but not be lead pastor.
   70 Women may fill any pastoral roles, including lead pastor.

19. **All things considered, would you prefer a woman or a man as your lead pastor?**

   2 A woman
   51 A man
   48 No preference

20. **Do you receive the Brethren magazine, *Messenger*, in your home?**

   67 No
   33 Yes

21. In your opinion, what is the ideal number of active members for a local congregation? *(write number)* about _____ active members

Median: **125** active members

22. How important is it to you that your local congregation is a part of the Church of the Brethren denomination?

  7 Not at all important
14 Not very important
40 Fairly important
40 Very important

23. In your view, how much priority should a pastor give to each of the following tasks? *(check one box for each task)*

	Low Priority	Medium Priority	High Priority	Top Priority
a. Preaching sermons	0	5	43	52
b. Planning and leading worship	4	21	51	25
c. Providing pastoral counseling and care	0	10	53	36
d. Managing conflict in the congregation	5	28	47	20
e. Visiting the sick	1	17	53	29
f. Teaching	8	34	42	17
g. Coordinating church programs	24	46	25	5
h. Equipping members for ministry	11	40	38	12
i. Shaping the congregation's vision	4	26	48	22
j. Leading local outreach programs	16	50	29	6
k. Being active in the larger Church of the Brethren	15	46	30	9
l. Being active in the broader ecumenical church	26	49	21	4
m. Emphasizing issues of peace and social justice	14	35	37	14
n. Supporting the world mission of the Church of the Brethren	10	36	39	15

24. In your view, what role should a church council (composed of the congregation's members) have in making decisions that affect the life of the congregation? *(check one)*

21 Council should decide <u>all</u> matters that affect the congregation.

41 Council should decide <u>most</u> matters that affect the congregation.

32 Council should decide only the <u>large</u> matters (e.g., choosing a pastor, making renovations, or approving budget).

6 Council should decide very little; most matters should be handled by the pastor and church board.

25. How much interest do you have in planting new churches? *(check one)*

45 I am not interested in planting churches.

39 I favor church planting, but I cannot do more than contribute money.

13 I would be willing to help plant a new church if I would not have to move.

3 I would be willing to move to another community to help plant a new church.

26. Should the Brethren have more, or less, emphasis on evangelism than at present?

47 More emphasis on evangelism

3 Less emphasis on evangelism

50 About the same as now

27. In which of these roles in your congregation, if any, could you accept a practicing homosexual? *(check all that apply)*

45 As a member

15 As a lay leader

11 As an ordained minister, if otherwise qualified

48 In none of these roles

28. How much do you agree or disagree with these statements? *(check one box for each statement)*

	Completely Disagree	Mostly Disagree	Mostly Agree	Completely Agree
a. My congregation has a clear sense of mission and purpose.	2	15	62	20
b. My relationship with my congregation is very important to me.	1	6	44	48
c. Worship services in my congregation inspire and strengthen me.	2	9	48	42
d. I feel personally supported by my congregation.	3	8	46	43
e. My congregation has experienced a great deal of conflict in the last five years.	19	39	27	16
f. The deacons play a vital role in my congregation.	4	16	54	27
g. My congregation has a strong commitment to serve the local community.	2	14	56	28
h. I favor ordaining women for pastoral ministry.	15	17	36	33

SECTION D: FAMILY LIFE AND BACKGROUND

1. Are you...

60 Female
40 Male

2. Which of these descriptions fit you? *(check all that apply)*

1 African American/Black
1 Asian or Pacific Islander
1 American Indian/Native American
0 Latino/Hispanic
94 White/Caucasian
1 Mixed racial/ethnic
1 Other *(write)* _____

3. Where were you born?

98 United States
2 Another country
(write) _____

4. In what year were you born?
(write year of birth) _____

13 Younger than 35 years old
23 35-49 years old
28 50-64 years old
36 65 or older

Median age: **57**

5. What was the first language that you learned as a child?

0 Spanish
98 English
1 Other *(write)* _____

120

6. **Where did you live when you were 12 years old?** *(check one)*

   36 On a farm
   21 In open country, but not on a farm
   25 In a small town (under 10,000) or its suburbs
   9 In a small city (10,000 to 50,000) or its suburbs
   6 In a medium city (50,000 to 250,000) or its suburbs
   4 In a large city (over 250,000) or its suburbs

7. **Where is your permanent residence now?**

   13 On a farm
   30 In open country, but not on a farm
   27 In a small town (under 10,000) or its suburbs
   14 In a small city (10,000 to 50,000) or its suburbs
   10 In a medium city (50,000 to 250,000) or its suburbs
   7 In a large city (over 250,000) or its suburbs

8. **How long have you lived in the general community where you now reside?**

   2 Less than 1 year
   8 1 to 4 years
   9 5 to 9 years
   18 10 to 20 years
   64 More than 20 years

9. **Do you currently live in a retirement community?**

   94 No
   6 Yes

10. **Have you ever lived outside of the United States for more than a two-month period?**

    88 No
    12 Yes

11. **Which is your current status?**

    9 Never married
    75 Married
    1 Separated
    5 Divorced
    10 Widowed
    0 Other (*write*)_____

12. **How many times, if any, have you been married?**
    (write the number) _____

    9 0
    76 Just once
    15 More than once

13. **How many times, if any, have you been divorced?**
    (write the number) _____

    82 0
    15 Just once
    3 More than once

14. **IF YOU WERE EVER MARRIED, did your most recent spouse grow up in a Brethren congregation?**

    60 No
    40 Yes

15. **IF YOU ARE MARRIED NOW, how happy has your marriage been for you?**

    5 Very unhappy
    2 Somewhat unhappy
    20 Somewhat happy
    74 Very happy

16. How happy was your family life for most of your childhood?

4 Very unhappy
8 Somewhat unhappy
47 Somewhat happy
41 Very happy

17. Did your parents divorce when you were growing up?

90 No
11 Yes

18. How many people live in your household? Count yourself and everyone who uses your home as their permanent address.
(write number) _____

Median: **2**
Mean: **2.5**[1]

19. How many children have you ever had, including those no longer living? *(write number)*

Biological children: _____
11 0
12 1
37 2
23 3
17 4+
Adopted children: _____
96 0
3 1
1 2
0 3
Step-children: _____
87 0
3 1
5 2
4 3+
TOTAL CHILDREN[2]
12 0
9 1
34 2
22 3
24 4+

20. IF YOU HAVE CHILDREN, how many still live with you for at least 2 months of the year?[3]
(write number) _____

62 0
15 1
16 2
8 3 or more

21. IF YOU EVER HAD CHILDREN, how much of the care did you typically provide for your children when they were under six years of age? Both men and women should answer. *(check one)*

2 None of it
10 Less than half
15 About half
26 Most of it
48 All of it

22. IF YOU EVER HAD CHILDREN, what was your employment status when your children were under six years of age? Both men and women should answer. *(check one)*

27 Not employed for pay
12 Employed part-time for pay
54 Employed full-time for pay
7 Other *(write)* _____

23. What is your <u>present</u> employment status? *(check all that apply)*

40 Employed full-time
11 Employed part-time
2 Unemployed
11 Homemaker
36 Retired
3 Student
5 Other *(write)* _____

24. How much of the household work like cleaning, washing, and cooking do you typically do in your home? *(circle a number on the scale from 0 to 10)*

3 0 = None
4 1
7 2
9 3
7 4
14 5 = Half
2 6
5 7
11 8
10 9
28 10 = All

25. How much of the property maintenance work (inside and outside) do you typically do in your home? *(circle a number on the scale from 0 to 10)*

9 0 = None
4 1
6 2
9 3
7 4
17 5 = Half
4 6
8 7
13 8
11 9
13 10 = All

26. How much do you agree or disagree with these statements? *(check one box for each statement)*

	Strongly Disagree	Disagree	Neither Agree nor Disagree	Agree	Strongly Agree
a. In a marriage, the woman's career should be as important as the man's.	3	9	25	36	27
b. The husband should have the "final say" in the family's decision making.	19	28	27	19	7
c. I prefer the new version of the Doxology, which avoids referring to God as "Father" or "Him."	43	26	24	6	3
d. Though it is not always possible, it is best if the wife stays at home and the husband works to support the family.	8	15	25	35	18

27. What is your <u>main</u> occupation? If retired, describe your <u>former</u> job.

_____

28. What <u>exactly</u> do you do at your job? _____

_____

29. IF YOU HAVE A SECOND JOB, what is your second job?

_____

30. In a typical week, about how many hours do you work for pay?

(write) _____ hours

- **37** 0
- **8** <20
- **13** 20-39
- **20** 40
- **22** >40

31. In a typical week, about how many hours do you spend doing any type of volunteer work outside of your congregation?

(write) _____ hours

- **60%** said "0" or didn't answer the question
- **32%** volunteer 2 hours or more per week

32. How good is your physical health on a scale from 1 to 10?

(circle a number between "very poor" and "very good")

| 1 = Very poor |
- **2** 1-2
- **6** 3-4
- **16** 5-6
- **38** 7-8
- **38** 9-10
| 10 = Very good |

33. Please indicate the level of formal education for each person below.

(Write a number beside each person. For students, indicate current level.)

Yourself	Your Spouse	Your Father	Your Mother	
3	4	33	25	Eighth grade or less
6	7	12	13	Some high school but did not graduate
32	35	30	37	High school graduate
10	11	5	4	Trade or technical school beyond high school
20	15	6	10	Some college, but not a four-year degree
12	14	6	6	College graduate, a four-year degree
5	3	1	1	Some graduate school, but not a degree
10	9	5	4	Master's or similar professional degree
3	2	2	0	Doctorate or similar advanced degree

34. Thinking about your own schooling in grades 1 through 12, how many years did you spend in each type of school below? *(write number of years, not including Kindergarten)*

6% of Brethren report having had some form of schooling outside of the public schools (whether in a private or home school setting).

94% received all of their primary and secondary education in the public schools.

35. Have you ever served in the armed forces or the National Guard?

88 No
12 Yes

IF YES, how long did you serve?

18 Less than 2 years
59 2 to 4 years
23 More than 4 years

36. How many members of your family have ever served in the Armed Forces? Include your parents, brothers and sisters, spouse, children, and yourself.

35 0
32 1
18 2
8 3
4 4
4 5 or more

37. WHETHER YOU ARE MALE OR FEMALE, if you were twenty years old and faced with a military draft, what position would you take?

32 Regular military service
30 Non-combatant military service
31 Alternative service (C.O.)
2 Register, but refuse induction or service
4 Refuse to register

38. Some people have felt unfairly treated by others in the church for various reasons. Did you ever feel unfairly treated by other Brethren for any of the following reasons? *(check all the apply)*

1 Because of my racial or ethnic status
2 Because of my sex or gender
2 Because of being unmarried
4 Because of being divorced
1 Because of my occupation
4 Because of my non-Brethren background
5 Because of my views related to peace and war
2 Because of my military service
1 Because of my sexual orientation

39. What is your sexual orientation?

98 Heterosexual
1 Bisexual
1 Homosexual
0 Other (*write*) _____

40. Have you ever experienced any type of sexual abuse or violation in your life? *(check all that apply)*

82 No, never
9 Yes, as a child
4 Yes, as a teenager
2 Yes, as an adult

41. Have you ever <u>lived</u> with someone in a romantic, but unmarried, relationship for a month or more?

81 No
19 Yes

SECTION E: BRETHREN MATTERS

1. Which of these, if any, have you done in your life? *(check all that apply)*

40 Attended a Church of the Brethren summer camp
5 Attended a Christian Citizenship Seminar
17 Attended NYC (National Youth Conference)
12 Volunteered at the Brethren Service Center in New Windsor, MD
3 Served in BVS (Brethren Volunteer Service)
1 Studied with Brethren Colleges Abroad (BCA)
4 Attended NOAC (National Older Adult Conference)
3 Attended a National Young Adult Conference
15 Helped with a Brethren Disaster Response project
5 Attended a Brethren Faith Expedition or Work Camp
2 Attended a Caring Ministry Assembly
38 Attended a Church of the Brethren District Conference
3 Studied at Bethany Theological Seminary
12 Served on a District board, council, or committee
14 Served on a denominational board, council, committee, or agency

2. Did you ever attend a Brethren-related college? (Percentage of total/percentage of those who attended college)[4]

89 / 77 No
4 / 7 Yes, but I did not graduate from one.
8 / 16 Yes, I graduated from a Brethren-related college.

IF YES, which Brethren-related college(s) did you attend?[5]

_____

_____

Bridgewater	**23%**
Elizabethtown	**10%**
Juniata	**6%**
Manchester	**42%**
McPherson	**16%**
La Verne	**3%**
Other	**2%**

3. How many times have you attended a Church of the Brethren Annual Conference?[6]

65 Never
12 Only once
6 2 times
4 3 times
3 4 times
10 5 or more times

4. **How many times have you served as a delegate to Annual Conference?**

   82 Never
   9 Only once
   3 2 times
   2 3 times
   1 4 times
   2 5 or more times

5. **How important are Annual Conference decisions and rulings to you personally?**

   18 Not at all important
   27 Not too important
   42 Fairly important
   14 Very important

6. **Should congregations that defy Annual Conference rulings be disciplined in some way, or should they be free to follow their own course?** *(check one)*

   10 They should be disciplined by the denomination.
   32 They should be counseled, but not disciplined.
   16 They should be free to follow their own course without outside interference.
   42 Not sure

7. **In your own experience, do you ever recall the Brethren disciplining a <u>member</u> who failed to live up to church standards?**

   75 No
   16 Yes
   10 Not sure

8. **Would you favor or oppose changing the name of the Church of the Brethren to a new name that does not include the word "Brethren"?**

   48 Strongly oppose
   27 Oppose
   3 Favor
   1 Strongly favor
   21 Not sure

9. **Should the Church of the Brethren be more, or less, active in world missions than at present?**

   34 Be more active in world missions
   3 Be less active in world missions
   63 Stay about the same as now

10. How satisfied are you, in general, with the program and emphases of each of the following agencies or groups? *(check one box for each agency)*[7]

	Not at All Satisfied	Not Very Satisfied	Fairly Satisfied	Very Satisfied	Not Sure
a. Church of the Brethren Annual Conference	1	5	37	19	38
b. Association of Brethren Caregivers (ABC)	1	1	24	18	57
c. Bethany Theological Seminary	2	5	25	19	49
d. Church of the Brethren General Board	1	3	34	19	44
e. On Earth Peace	2	4	23	17	53
f. Church of the Brethren Washington Office	1	3	19	10	68
g. Brethren Disaster Response	0	1	24	43	31
h. The Brethren Service Center in New Windsor	0	1	19	32	48
i. Brethren Benefit Trust (BBT)	0	3	16	10	71
j. Brethren Pension Plan	0	2	16	9	72
k. Brethren Insurance Plans	2	4	14	8	71
l. Brethren Foundation	0	1	16	7	76
m. Church of the Brethren Credit Union	0	1	12	6	80
n. Church of the Brethren General Offices in Elgin	1	4	24	14	57
o. The Brethren/Mennonite Council for Gay and Lesbian Concerns	11	5	8	5	71
p. Brethren Revival Fellowship	1	4	19	12	64
q. Womaen's Caucus	2	3	13	6	76
r. The Brethren Encyclopedia, Inc.	0	1	13	8	77
s. Outdoor Ministries Association	0	1	17	13	69
t. The World Council of Churches	5	6	20	11	58

11. How important are these ministries of the Church of the Brethren to you?

	Not at All Important	Not Very Important	Fairly Important	Very Important
a. Working for peace and justice	2	7	45	46
b. Offering a distinctive Brethren witness to the world	3	15	50	32
c. Offering a message of salvation to the secular culture	2	9	42	47
d. Service and disaster relief	0	2	37	61
e. Equipping members for ministry	1	7	45	46
f. Partnering with other Christian denominations	2	10	56	32
g. Sharing God's love in word and deed	0	2	22	76
h. Calling and training pastors	1	6	44	49

12. As you think about the church in general, how strong is your <u>personal commitment</u> to each of the following bodies? *(check one box for each statement)*

	Very Weak	Somewhat Weak	Somewhat Strong	Very Strong
a. Your local congregation	5	12	30	54
b. Your own District of the Church of the Brethren	15	29	40	16
c. The Church of the Brethren nationally	21	32	34	13
d. The broader Christian Church	16	26	39	19

13. "Continuing the work of Jesus, peacefully, simply, and together," is often used to describe the Church of the Brethren. Please rank from 1 to 4 the importance of each part of this phrase. *(Place a different number beside each word.)*

	Least Important	3rd Most Important	2nd Most Important	Most Important
Continuing the work of Jesus	6	3	4	87
Peacefully	13	33	39	15
Simply	52	25	17	6
Together	17	25	44	13

14. Which of the following have you ever done <u>for religious reasons</u>? *(check all that apply)*

- **39** Worn a covering or prayer veil
- **1** Grown a beard
- **28** Fasted
- **9** Refrained from wearing an item of jewelry
- **2** Refrained from wearing a necktie
- **19** "Affirmed" rather than swearing an oath in court

15. To the best of your knowledge when was the church of the Brethren founded?

- **2** 1589
- **39** 1708
- **13** 1789
- **7** 1881
- **1** 1939
- **39** No idea

16. Which statement <u>best</u> reflects your understanding of the Church of the Brethren's position on creeds? *(check one)*

- **9** The church has an official creed, which it expects members to learn and to follow.
- **16** The church expects people to accept certain doctrines in order to become members.
- **61** The church accepts the entire New Testament as its rule of faith and practice.
- **14** The church is non-creedal; individuals are free to arrive at their own faith understandings.

17. When you are in a situation where everyone is asked to repeat the pledge of allegiance, what do you typically do?

- **87** I repeat the pledge without hesitation.
- **7** I repeat the pledge with some hesitation and discomfort.
- **2** I mouth the words of the pledge, without really saying it.
- **5** I do not repeat the pledge of allegiance.

18. How much do you agree or disagree with each of these statements?
(check one box for each statement)

	Strongly Disagree	Disagree	Neither Agree nor Disagree	Agree	Strongly Agree
a. In its adjustment to modern society, the Church of the Brethren has lost valuable parts of its heritage and tradition.	2	17	39	35	7
b. The Church of the Brethren should make some provision for baptizing infants.	28	35	24	10	2
c. It is wrong to help in any war by fighting.	13	31	31	17	9
d. The Church of the Brethren should provide for its members a set of concrete guidelines for Christian living.	6	25	35	28	5
e. Brethren should <u>not</u> initiate lawsuits.	4	20	41	28	6[8]
f. Brethren should <u>not</u> vote in national elections.	55	35	8	1	1
g. Brethren young persons should be counseled <u>not</u> to join the armed forces.	18	33[9]	30	14	4
h. Annual Conference is too expensive to hold every year.	6	22	56	13	3
i. It is all right for Brethren to live the same lifestyle as other Americans.	11	32	31	21	4
j. The Church of the Brethren would be better off if it paid more attention to its similarities with other groups and less to its differences.	4	18	47	28	4
k. Complete nonviolence as a way of living is very important to me.	4	16	26	41	13
l. The Brethren community has no right to challenge the way I live.	5	33	38	20	4
m. Divorce is preferable to maintaining an unhappy marriage.	7	20	33	33	7
n. Interracial marriages are morally wrong.	24	28	29	14	5

19. How much, if any, conflict do you experience between your personal beliefs and practices and those of the larger society?

16 No conflict
26 Little conflict
45 Some conflict
13 Much conflict

20. How much, if any, conflict do you experience between Church of the Brethren beliefs and practices and those of the larger society?

16 No conflict
27 Little conflict
48 Some conflict
9 Much conflict

21. Which statement best expresses your future relationship with the Church of the Brethren?
(check one)

26 I will always want to remain a member of the Church of the Brethren and could never feel right being a member of another denomination.

45 Although I prefer the Church of the Brethren, there are some other churches that I could feel comfortable in.

23 I could be just as happy in certain other churches as in the Church of the Brethren.

2 I often feel that I could be happier in a non-Brethren church.

2 I have definite thoughts of joining a non-Brethren church.

1 I am considering discontinuing membership in any church.

22. Is there any important way in which the Church of the Brethren seems different to you from other Protestant denominations such as the Methodists or Presbyterians?

43 Yes
47 Not really
4 Not at all
5 Opted out[10]

IF YES, please explain how Brethren seem different. _____
_____
_____
_____

SECTION F: FAITH AND SOCIAL ISSUES

1. **When you think about the way most Americans lived 100 years ago compared to today, which statement best reflects your general outlook?** *(check one)*

   8 Life was definitely better 100 years ago.

   30 Life is probably as good now as then; each generation has its good and bad.

   45 Life is probably better now, even though some good things have been lost.

   17 Life is definitely better now than 100 years ago.

2. **Do you think the U.S. government is spending too much, too little, or about the right amount to protect the environment?**

   12 Too much

   55 Too little

   32 About the right amount

3. **On the whole, do you think immigration—people coming from other countries to live here in the United States—is a good thing or a bad thing?**

   6 A very bad thing

   44 More bad than good

   44 More good than bad

   6 A very good thing

4. **Do you think that a person with an incurable disease has the right to end his or her own life?**

   51 No

   19 Yes

   30 Not sure

5. **How important is it to you that Brethren leaders discuss and address issues of race and racism?**

   7 Not important at all

   20 Not very important

   46 Fairly important

   26 Very important

6. **Some people think there should be intentional efforts to hire and promote racial/ethnic minorities to overcome patterns of racism in our society. Do you favor or oppose such efforts?**

   13 Strongly oppose

   46 Oppose

   37 Favor

   4 Strongly favor

7. **Which description best reflects your general outlook on the abortion issue?** *(check one)*

   47 Strongly pro-life

   15 Moderately pro-life

   17 Neutral

   14 Moderately pro-choice

   8 Strongly pro-choice

8. **Which of these statements best describes your feelings about abortion?** *(check one)*

   56 Abortion is just as bad as killing a person who has already been born; it is murder.

   9 Abortion is murder, but it is not as bad as killing someone who has already been born.

   25 Abortion is not murder, but it does involve the taking of human life.

   10 Abortion is not murder; it is a surgical procedure for removing human tissue.

9. **Do you generally think of yourself as a Republican, Democrat, Independent, or something else?**

   51 Republican
   25 Democrat
   13 Independent
   0 Some other political party
   10 No party

10. **Who did you vote for in the 2004 presidential election?**

    62 George W. Bush
    25 John Kerry
    2 Someone else
    11 I did not vote for president.

11. **IF YOU VOTED, how much did your religious beliefs affect your vote?**

    12 Not at all
    17 Not very much
    38 A fair amount
    33 A great deal

12. **Which best describes your overall political beliefs?**

    10 Very conservative
    43 Conservative
    35 Moderate
    10 Liberal
    2 Very liberal

13. People have different views of the behaviors listed below. Please indicate how wrong you consider each behavior to be. *(check one box for each behavior)*

	Never Wrong	Rarely Wrong	Sometimes Wrong	Usually Wrong	Always Wrong
a. Divorce	2	5	52	35	5
b. Remarriage after divorce	15	24	43	11	6
c. Drinking alcohol	2	7	37	27	27
d. Marriage between a Christian and a non-Christian	10	14	39	24	13
e. Couples living together before marriage	3	6	17	23	51
f. Smoking marijuana	1	1	5	17	76
g. Smoking cigarettes	1	2	7	21	68
h. Watching X-rated (adult) movies	1	2	7	17	73
i. Premarital sex	1	3	14	22	60
j. Extramarital sex	0	0	2	7	90
k. Homosexual relations between consenting adults	4	5	8	8	75
l. Investing stock in companies that profit from defense, gambling, tobacco or alcohol	2	5	22	32	39
m. Entering the armed forces	24	23	33	14	6
n. Telling a lie	0	1	10	33	56
o. Gambling	1	2	20	28	48
p. Taking prescription medications to reduce anxiety	15	27	43	11	3
q. Buying stylish and fashionable clothing	12	29	47	8	3
r. Working as a police officer	54	32	11	2	1
s. Buying government lottery tickets	8	13	25	20	34
t. Dancing	33	30	29	5	3
u. Copying a music CD for a friend	12	17	23	24	24
v. Profanity (cursing)	1	3	10	23	63
w. Spanking children	9	20	52	12	7
x. Viewing pornographic materials	1	2	7	14	76
y. Buying a $50,000 sports car	6	8	35	24	27
z. Abortion	1	4	19	25	52

14. **On a 1 to 6 scale, where 1 means "American citizen," and 6 means "citizen of the world," do you tend to identify yourself more as an American or as a citizen of the world?** *(circle a number)*

    58 1 = American citizen
    13 2
    11 3
    6 4
    7 5
    4 6 = A citizen of the world

15. **Some people think America impacts the rest of the world in very positive ways while others see our influence as more negative. On the following 7 point scale, how would you rate America's overall impact upon the rest of the world?**

    1 1 = Completely negative
    6 2
    14 3
    26 4 = Neutral
    31 5
    18 6
    5 7 = Completely positive

16. **How much do you agree or disagree with these statements?** *(check one box for each statement)*

	Completely Disagree	Mostly Disagree	Mostly Agree	Completely Agree
a. America is a Christian nation.	5	22	64	9
b. The "War on Terror" is a religious battle between the forces of good and evil.	17	25	43	15
c. It is all right to display the American flag inside a Brethren sanctuary.	12	16	31	41
d. The U.S. did the right thing by going to war in Iraq.	27	25	34	13
e. The U.S. armed forces should continue the fight against terror until all serious threats have been eliminated.	16	23	42	19
f. The United States has a special role in God's plan for the world.	11	16	47	25

17. How patriotic would you say that you are?

- **2** Not patriotic at all
- **9** Not very patriotic
- **53** Moderately patriotic
- **36** Very patriotic

18. Some people believe that God blesses America in a special way. Which statement best expresses your view? *(check one)*

- **9** God does not bless nations.
- **47** God blesses all nations.
- **43** God has especially blessed America.
- **1** God blesses other nations more than America.

19. Which statement best reflects how you think Christians should relate to government? *(check one)*

- **2** Avoid government and politics as much as possible
- **10** Cooperate as needed but do not get too involved
- **55** Try to influence government to do what is right
- **33** Actively participate in government to improve it

20. Do you favor or oppose the death penalty for persons convicted of murder?

- **13** Strongly oppose
- **19** Oppose
- **28** Neither favor nor oppose
- **30** Favor
- **9** Strongly favor

21. How much do you agree or disagree with these statements? *(check one box for each statement)*

	Completely Disagree	Mostly Disagree	Mostly Agree	Completely Agree
a. America is a force for good in the world.	3	13	70	15
b. America often tramples upon the rights of other nations.	7	46	38	10
c. The world would be better off if more nations embraced Christianity.	2	8	34	56
d. The world would be better off if more nations embraced American values.	6	33	52	9
e. The U.S. should admit more immigrants from the rest of the world.	18	54	26	2
f. America should help Americans first, and the rest of the world later.	6	29	50	16
g. The U.S. should remain the world's dominant military power.	8	19	54	20
h. American culture is superior to most other cultures.	12	35	45	8
i. America should spend more time listening, and less time telling other nations what to do.	2	18	57	22

22. In our country today, homosexuality is a hotly contested issue with Americans having strong feelings on both sides. How much do you agree or disagree with these statements?

	Completely Disagree	Mostly Disagree	Mostly Agree	Completely Agree
a. Homosexual couples—that is, couples of the same sex— should have the right to marry.	71	12	8	8
b. Homosexual couples should be allowed to adopt children.	63	17	12	8
c. Homosexual behavior should be against the law, even if it occurs between consenting adults.	38	25	14	22
d. A person is born either a homosexual or a heterosexual, and there is little they can do to change it.	45	26	20	9
e. Homosexuality should be considered an acceptable alternative lifestyle.	60	17	13	9

SECTION G: LIFESTYLE AND STEWARDSHIP

1. About how often do you do the activities below?
(check one box for each activity)

	Never	Rarely	Several Times a Month	Several Times a Week	Daily
a. Listen to Christian radio stations	13	33	18	17	18
b. Listen to *Focus on the Family*	39	31	14	11	5
c. Listen to *National Public Radio*	29	32	14	13	13
d. Watch religious programs on TV	12	36	31	15	6
e. Watch sports events on TV	12	34	30	19	6
f. Watch *MTV* or *Comedy Central* on TV	53	30	9	6	2
g. Read newspapers or magazines	1	8	16	22	53
h. Read books	3	22	24	21	30
i. Watch Christian videos	18	53	21	6	2
j. Watch movies (at home or in a theater)	5	38	39	14	5

2. **About what portion of your household income do you give to church and charitable causes?**

   7 Less than 1 percent
   21 1 to 5 percent
   21 6 to 9 percent
   31 10 percent
   17 11 to 20 percent
   2 More than 20 percent

3. **About how many dollars a <u>month</u> do you give in congregational offerings?**
   (write number) $_____

4. **During the past two years has your household giving to your local congregation increased or decreased?**

   40 Increased
   11 Decreased
   45 Stayed about the same
   4 Not sure

5. **To which of the following have you made a direct monetary contribution during the past two years?** *(check all that apply)*

   5 On Earth Peace
   26 Habitat for Humanity
   6 Focus on the Family
   32 Heifer Project International
   5 Bethany Theological Seminary
   15 Church of the Brethren General Board
   4 Association of Brethren Caregivers
   10 A Brethren-related college
   25 A Church of the Brethren camp
   40 Brethren Disaster Response
   12 A Brethren retirement community or nursing home

6. **During the past two years has your household giving to Brethren-related agencies increased or decreased?**

   15 Increased
   9 Decreased
   60 Stayed about the same
   17 Not sure

7. **Based on what you know about the work of Brethren-related agencies, how satisfied are you with how they use the money contributed to them?**

   14 Very satisfied
   56 Satisfied
   28 I have mixed feelings.
   2 Dissatisfied
   1 Very dissatisfied

8. **Generally speaking, how do direct mail solicitations from Brethren-related agencies affect your giving to those agencies?**

   1 Increase it greatly
   9 Increase it somewhat
   6 Decrease it
   84 Have little effect either way

9. **Do you rent or own your home?**

   11 Rent
   90 Own

   IF YOU OWN, what is your home's approximate market value?

   11 Under $75,000
   14 $75,000 to $99,000
   24 $100,000 to $149,000
   19 $150,000 to $199,000
   19 $200,000 to $299,000
   7 $300,000 to $399,00
   4 $400,000 to $499,000
   3 $500,000 or more

10. **In which group did the total income for all members of your HOUSEHOLD fall in 2005?** Give your best estimate of all sources of income before taxes or other deductions.

    2 Under $5,000
    7 $5,000 to $14,999
  13 $15,000 to $24,999
  17 $25,000 to $39,999
  12 $40,000 to $49,999
  24 $50,000 to $74,999
  13 $75,000 to $99,999
    9 $100,000 to $149,999
    2 $150,000 to $199,999
    1 $200,000 to $250,000
    1 More than $250,000

11. **How many of the following items are presently in your household?** *(write a number for EACH item)*[11]

  2.0 Televisions
  1.2 Cell phones
  0.2 Hand guns
  0.7 Hunting rifles
  1.0 DVD players
  0.1 Large screen TVs
  0.9 Personal computers
  0.3 Video game systems
  1.8 Cars, SUVs, vans, trucks
  0.0 Motor homes

For distributions see this endnote:[12]

12. **Taking all things together, how happy would you say you are in general?**

    2 Not too happy
  44 Fairly happy
  56 Very happy

13. **In a typical day, about how many hours do you watch television?**
(write) _____ hours

Median: **2** hours
Mean: **2½** hours[13]

14. **What type of Internet access do you have in your home?**

  35 None
  37 Dial-up connection
  29 High speed connection

15. **In a typical day, about how many hours do you use the Internet at home?** Include all activities such as e-mail, instant messaging, chat rooms, shopping, and browsing.
(write) _____ hours

Median: **¼** hour
Mean: **½** hour[14]

16. **Which of the following activities do you do on the Internet?** *(check all that apply)*

  29 Buy things
    5 Contribute to charities
  22 Banking
  56 Use e-mail
  14 Send instant messages (IM)
  31 Read news
  18 Receive news about the church
  15 Search for religious information

17. **How much stress do you typically feel from the pace and complexity of daily life?**

    7 None
  36 A little bit
  39 A fair amount
  13 Pretty much
    5 Very much

18. **Whether you are a player or a fan, how important are sports in your life?**

    25 Not at all important
    40 Not very important
    30 Fairly important
     5 Very important

19. **In the past <u>year</u>, about how often did you do each of the following things, if at all?** *(check one box for each activity)*

	Never	Rarely	Several Times a Month	Several Times a Week	Daily
a. Engaged in active physical exercise	5	21	21	35	18
b. Saw an X-rated (adult) movie	88	11	1	0	0
c. Bought tickets in a state lottery	63	27	7	2	0
d. Assisted neighbors in need	3	32	53	9	2
e. Drank alcohol	50	33	12	4	1
f. Displayed a U.S. flag outside your home	42	22	13	3	19
g. Visited a therapist for counseling	90	7	3	0	0
h. Taken prescription medication for anxiety or depression	79	6	2	2	11
i. Recycled products to protect the environment	12	18	24	11	35
j. Practiced yoga	91	6	2	1	1
k. Visited pornographic websites	93	6	1	0	0
l. Followed a healthy diet	3	15	18	29	36

20. **As you think about important issues facing Brethren churches today, what <u>two</u> issues concern you the most?**

    1. _____

    2. _____

Survey endnotes

[1] Mean trimmed by 10% on both sides to provide more robust estimate of typical response.

[2] Modified estimate, that assumes that respondents who reported being single <u>and</u> never married, and who failed to respond to the entire section reporting number of children, skipped over it because they have had no children.

[3] Same assumption in effect as in question D 19 (previous endnote).

[4] Additional breakdown of attendance at a Brethren college by age group. Percentages for each age group are the percentage of the college educated respondents who attended a Brethren college.

	<35	35-49	50-64	65 or older	Total	N
No	86.6	81.8	74.6	63.7	76.6	644.5
Yes, but didn't graduate	4.4	3.5	9.4	11.9	7.3	61.6
Yes, Graduated	9.0	14.7	16.1	24.4	16.1	135.8
Total	100.0	100.0	100.0	100.0	100.0	
N	173.2	228.6	250.3	189.7		841.8

[5] Additional breakdown of attendance at various Brethren colleges by age group. Percentages for each age group are the percentage of college educated respondents who attended each college.

	<35	35-49	50-64	65 or older	Total	N
Non-Brethren College	87.9	84.8	79.6	72.9	81.2	698.4
Bridgewater	6.3	2.7	3.8	5.0	4.3	36.9
Elizabethtown	0.0	1.9	2.1	3.2	1.9	16.2
Juniata	0.4	0.9	1.1	1.9	1.1	9.3
Manchester	3.0	5.5	10.1	11.8	7.8	66.9
McPherson	1.8	3.5	3.1	3.6	3.0	26.2
La Verne	0.0	0.3	0.0	1.7	0.5	4.0
Other	0.5	0.4	0.3	0.0	0.3	2.6
Total	100.0	100.0	100.0	100.0	100.0	
N	174.5	232.0	258.3	195.9		860.6

[6] The percentages for E3 and E4 assume that those who didn't answer the question have never attended or served as an Annual Conference delegate. The percentages for E5 assume that nonrespondents see Annual Conference as not at all important. The percentages for E6 add nonrespondents to the "Not sure" category.

[7] The percentages for this series are adjusted to reflect the "nonresponse" of many who systematically neglected to respond to this particular series. Respondents who answered the name change question, two questions prior to this series, and

who left unanswered more than one item in this list, were included in the "Not sure" category, the reasoning being that they were skipping items due to lack of knowledge or salience, and thus were "Not sure" how to respond. The large number of nonrespondents to this series prompted this adjustment. To have left the percentages as they were, would have systematically exaggerated the percent of respondents who provided answers other than "not sure."

[8] Including the decimals, the "agrees" here add up to 35%, not 34%.

[9] Including the decimals, the "disagrees" here add up to 52%, not 51%.

[10] Those who "opted out" are those who answered the previous question, but omitted this one.

[11] Trimmed means reported (10% trimmed from each side of distribution before computing the mean).

[12] Frequency distributions for household consumption items — How many of the following items are presently in your household? ...

Number of televisions in household	Frequency	Cumulative Frequency	Percent	Cumulative Percent
0	16.3	16.3	0.9	0.9
1	270.2	286.5	15.6	16.5
1.1	393.1	679.7	22.7	39.2
2	491.3	1171.0	28.3	67.5
3	312.5	1483.5	18.0	85.5
4	166.0	1649.5	9.6	95.1
5	57.4	1706.9	3.3	98.4
6	15.1	1722.0	0.9	99.3
7	8.4	1730.4	0.5	99.8
8	1.7	1732.0	0.1	99.9
9	2.1	1734.2	0.1	100.0

Number of cell phones in household	Frequency	Cumulative Frequency	Percent	Cumulative Percent
0	381.2	381.2	22.0	22.0
1	441.3	822.5	25.5	47.6
1.1	291.6	1114.1	16.9	64.4
2	419.5	1533.6	24.3	88.7
3	117.2	1650.8	6.8	95.4
4	60.9	1711.7	3.5	99.0
5	13.9	1725.5	0.8	99.8
6	1.1	1726.7	0.1	99.8
7	1.9	1728.6	0.1	99.9
9	1.1	1729.7	0.1	100.0

Number of hand guns in household	Frequency	Cumulative Frequency	Percent	Cumulative Percent
0	1216.3	1216.3	70.6	70.6
1	202.1	1418.5	11.7	82.4
1.1	131.2	1549.6	7.6	90.0
2	99.0	1648.6	5.7	95.7
3	35.1	1683.7	2.0	97.8
4	6.9	1690.6	0.4	98.2
5	9.5	1700.0	0.5	98.7
6	9.8	1709.8	0.6	99.3
7	3.1	1712.9	0.2	99.5
8	1.3	1714.2	0.1	99.5
9	7.8	1722.1	0.5	100.0

Number of hunting rifles in household	Frequency	Cumulative Frequency	Percent	Cumulative Percent
0	918.9	918.9	53.4	53.4
1	177.5	1096.4	10.3	63.7
1.1	198.4	1294.9	11.5	75.2
2	126.6	1421.5	7.4	82.6
3	83.3	1504.8	4.8	87.4
4	63.3	1568.2	3.7	91.1
5	30.5	1598.7	1.8	92.9
6	40.2	1638.9	2.3	95.2
7	10.4	1649.3	0.6	95.8
8	17.4	1666.7	1.0	96.9
9	54.1	1720.8	3.1	100.0

Number of DVD players in household	Frequency	Cumulative Frequency	Percent	Cumulative Percent
0	383.0	383.0	22.1	22.1
1	652.9	1035.9	37.8	59.9
1.1	288.7	1324.6	16.7	76.6
2	280.4	1605.0	16.2	92.8
3	92.2	1697.1	5.3	98.1
4	22.1	1719.3	1.3	99.4
5	6.8	1726.1	0.4	99.8
6	1.8	1727.9	0.1	99.9
7	1.6	1729.5	0.1	100.0

Number of large screen TV's in household	Frequency	Cumulative Frequency	Percent	Cumulative Percent
0	1420.6	1420.6	82.4	82.4
1	209.6	1630.1	12.2	94.5
1.1	75.5	1705.7	4.4	98.9
2	16.0	1721.7	0.9	99.8
3	1.6	1723.3	0.1	99.9
9	1.1	1724.4	0.1	100.0

Number of personal computers in household	Frequency	Cumulative Frequency	Percent	Cumulative Percent
0	473.0	473.0	27.4	27.4
1	655.3	1128.3	38.0	65.4
1.1	257.6	1385.8	14.9	80.3
2	238.0	1623.9	13.8	94.1
3	67.9	1691.8	3.9	98.1
4	25.0	1716.8	1.4	99.5
5	4.3	1721.0	0.2	99.8
6	1.8	1722.9	0.1	99.9
7	1.0	1723.8	0.1	99.9
9	1.1	1725.0	0.1	100.0

Number of video game systems in household	Frequency	Cumulative Frequency	Percent	Cumulative Percent
0	1184.2	1184.2	68.7	68.7
1	292.4	1476.5	17.0	85.7
1.1	113.0	1589.5	6.6	92.3
2	88.2	1677.7	5.1	97.4
3	33.0	1710.6	1.9	99.3
4	6.2	1716.8	0.4	99.7
5	3.3	1720.2	0.2	99.9
9	2.6	1722.7	0.1	100.0

Number of motor vehicles in household	Frequency	Cumulative Frequency	Percent	Cumulative Percent
0	85.2	85.2	4.9	4.9
1	252.4	337.5	14.6	19.5
1.1	354.6	692.1	20.5	40.0
2	614.4	1306.6	35.5	75.6
3	268.3	1574.9	15.5	91.1
4	89.5	1664.4	5.2	96.3
5	46.2	1710.6	2.7	99.0
6	10.0	1720.5	0.6	99.5
7	3.2	1723.7	0.2	99.7
9	4.9	1728.6	0.3	100.0

Number of motor homes in household	Frequency	Cumulative Frequency	Percent	Cumulative Percent
0	1643.5	1643.5	95.5	95.5
1	49.6	1693.1	2.9	98.4
1.1	22.4	1715.6	1.3	99.7
2	0.7	1716.2	0.0	99.7
3	2.6	1718.8	0.2	99.9
4	0.9	1719.7	0.1	99.9
9	1.1	1720.9	0.1	100.0

[13] Approximate value of trimmed mean. Trimmed mean (10% trimmed from each side) = 2.53 hours.

[14] Approximate value of trimmed mean. Trimmed mean (10% trimmed from each side) = .455 hours.